"I Think I'll Just Go
On Anyway"

"I Think I'll Just Go On Anyway"

By Dr. Raymond Hancock

Sword of the Lord Publishers
Murfreesboro, Tennessee 37130

Printed in the United States of America

Introduction

"See it through!" "Don't quit!" we preachers admonish. The purpose of this volume of sermons is to motivate and encourage Christians to overcome every obstacle, and never give up or slack up, but march through the Christian life in victory.

It is my joy and honor to say a brief word of introduction for these encouraging messages by my friend, Dr. Raymond Hancock.

I first met Raymond Hancock in 1973 when he was pastor of Providence Baptist Church in Tampa, Florida. There he built a great church and served as pastor nineteen years. He has been the pastor of Pinecrest Baptist Church in Morrow, Georgia, for five years, building the average Sunday school attendance from less than 800 to a high attendance of more than 1,400. During his ministry at Pinecrest, the missions program has increased to include support of one hundred missionaries. Pinecrest is a growing, enthusiastic, soul-winning church. It has been my privilege to speak at both Providence Baptist Church and Pinecrest Baptist Church. Raymond Hancock is a great pastor, a soul winner and a builder of Christians.

This book contains messages that will give you courage and resolution. It will cheer you and give you new confidence. The discouraged, it will strengthen.

The Saviour taught us that good preaching uses the things at hand to illustrate. Dr. Hancock ably uses the same approach illustrating from his own life with modern incidents and current phrases.

This is preaching to bless Christians and instruct them how to live.

My sincere prayer is that God will use these messages to inspire others to "just go on anyway."

Dr. Curtis Hutson
Editor, SWORD OF THE LORD

Forword

The chapters in this book are chapters out of my life and ministry. My life's text is Isaiah 40:31, *"But they that wait upon the Lord shall renew their strength; they shall mount up with wings as eagles; they shall run, and not be weary; and they shall walk, and not faint."* Among the difficulties and disappointments along the Christian's pathway, I have found that our wonderful Lord can lift us up and give us victory.

In this book, I share with you the many ways in which He has helped me and the wonderful people I have had the joy and privilege of pastoring.

I owe a special and eternal debt of gratitude to my Lord and to my faithful wife and companion. God used her so many times to help me soar higher in my Christian life and ministry. To the wonderful people of Pinecrest Baptist Church, I owe so much. All of these messages have been preached to them over a period of five years. It has been thrilling to see them mount up and grow and go forward as a great company of saints for our Lord and Saviour.

My prayer is that the Lord will be able to use this book to help you soar in your Christian life.

Raymond L. Hancock

Table of Contents

CHAPTER 1

"*I Think I'll Just Go On Anyway*"

I want to speak to you tonight from chapter 6 of the book of Hebrews on the subject, "I Think I'll Just Go On Anyway." Have you ever thought about quitting? Have you ever thought about giving up? Have you ever thought about throwing in the towel? Some folks have. There was a time when I didn't know which way to go, or what to do. It was a very low time.

Yes, preachers are human; and preachers have problems. Preachers have troubles and trials and loads to carry. There was a great trying time in my ministry. I think the Lord allowed me to go through it so I could sympathize with others who sometimes get down on the bottom.

As I sat in my office thinking about what to do, or if I should do anything, the thought came to me, "This is not the time to quit! In spite of everything, I'll just go on anyway! I'll believe God; I'll trust the Lord; I'll pray and preach and just go on anyway."

That is what I want to preach about: "I Think I'll Just Go On Anyway."

Look at Hebrews, chapter 6. I am going to lift this text out of its context and use the thought that Paul used when he encouraged believers to go on. The believers were at a place, and they needed to go on. Verse 1:

"Therefore leaving the principles of the doctrine of Christ, let us go on unto perfection; not laying again the foundation of repentance from dead works, and of faith toward God."

Paul was not saying that we ought to forget doctrine, that we ought to forget Scripture, because we never do that. We always must hold fast to the things that we believe are true and right. We always must hold fast to the fundamentals of the Faith. But there is a sense in which we need to move on in our Christian lives. So he said to move on, "not laying again the foundation of repentance. . . ."

There are some things you can do only once. You can only be saved one time. You can only one time lay the foundation of repentance for salvation. Now, you can repent many times; but you can but one time repent and have faith for salvation. Some things you cannot do over again; you just have to go on from there.

Paul was saying here that you need to go on from these first principles of faith in Christ and salvation. Go on and perfect that which the Lord has given to us.

When he says, ". . .let us go on unto perfection," he is not saying, ". . .let us go on until we reach the stage of sinless perfection," for that is impossible. There is only one perfect person—the Lord Jesus Christ. You and I have a battle, a war, a fight going on all the time. Paul said, "When I would do good, evil is present." But we ought to go on unto perfection.

I. GO ON IN SPITE OF OPPOSITION

We should, however, go on perfecting the life and ministry that the Lord has given to us. Whatever God has done for you, or called you to do, you ought to seek to perfect that ministry. God has called me to preach. So I ought to seek and be busy about perfecting the ministry of preaching. If God has called you to teach, to be a bus pastor, or to do some other ministry, then seek to perfect that ministry.

Set your sights on nothing less than the best. When you realize what God wants you to do, then set your sights, as did the Apostle Paul when he said, "I press toward the mark." He had a mark out there. He knew where he was going. He knew where he ought to wind up, and he said, ". . .looking unto Jesus, the author and the finisher of our faith." Seek to perfect that ministry and that Christian life.

Furthermore, seek to be the very best Christian you can be. Not a mediocre, not an average, not a run-of-the-mill Christian, but the very best Christian in your town or community. Be the best Christian in your church. Be the best Christian that some lost man knows. Seek to perfect your Christian ministry and your Christian life.

Instead of studying to see how good a Christian they can be, and how perfect they can be in their Christian life, some are trying to see how much they can get by with, or how little they can do and still be a Christian.

Well, when we set our sights on what we ought to be and determine in our hearts what we ought to do, then problems inevitably arise. But be determined about it. When that desire gets hold on your heart and you set your sights to start out, there will be opposition.

You cannot be a good Christian without opposition. Neither can you be a good preacher without opposition. You cannot be a good deacon, a good bus captain, without opposition. You cannot be a good anything without opposition. The Devil will do everything he can to keep you from being all you ought to be for God.

We can all wish there were no opposition. In the business world, I am sure the businessman could wish there were no such thing as opposition; but there is opposition in business, opposition in sports, opposition everywhere. But believers in the Lord Jesus Christ should know that we face the greatest opposition in the world.

The Bible tells us in Ephesians 6:12, "For we wrestle not against flesh and blood, but against principalities, against powers, against the rulers of the darkness of this world. . . ." All Hell is against us to keep us from being what we ought to be for God. There is always opposition to good and right. All Hell is out to stop me from preaching. All Hell is out to stop you from being what you ought to be for the Lord. There is and always will be opposition. But Paul said, ". . .let us go on."

If we get to where we are going, if we wind up victorious, if we realize the victory, it will be through opposition. There will be many times when we will have to say, "It doesn't matter; I'm going on anyway." You will be tempted to give up that bus route or that Bible class or quit being a deacon or usher, even quit being a preacher. Just QUIT, QUIT!! But we will have to say, "No, I think I'll just go on anyway."

If you do, it will be—

II. IN SPITE OF EVERY TEST.

You are going to be tested. If your aim is pure and your desire is real, you are going to be tested. It is easy to walk down the aisle; it is easy to feel good in your heart and soul when the preacher is preaching. In the midst of a great revival meeting, you may feel a desire to serve God. You may determine to serve the Lord. Possibly when you hear a Bible message, you determine to start reading your Bible, to start praying like you have never prayed, to go witnessing, and to keep at it.

But once you let desire stir up and kindle a fire in your heart, you will be put to the test to see just how sincere that desire really is. You will not say, "I'm going soul winning," before there will be opposition to keep you from going soul winning. You will not say, "I'm going to pray," until there will be opposition to keep you from praying. Yes, there will be tests to see if you are going to fulfill that desire.

Turn with me to Nehemiah. Most of you know the story of Nehemiah. In chapter 2, Nehemiah was the king's cupbearer. Furthermore, he had a burning desire to do something for God, a ministry, something to perfect for the Lord. In Nehemiah 1:3, Nehemiah received word concerning Jerusalem that the walls and the gates were burned with fire. Verse 4 says this broke Nehemiah's heart, and he mourned and fasted for certain days. (We, too, ought to mourn and fast when there is work that needs to be done for God.)

Something began to boil up, to burn, in Nehemiah. He had the desire to do something. So he came before the king the next day. Now look at chapter 2 and verse 2: The king looked at him and said, 'Why are you so sad today? Why is your countenance sad? You are not sick.' Nehemiah answered the king: "Why should not my countenance be sad? Back over at the home place the walls of God and the gates that swung open wide to the city, the walls that once stood as a testimony, have been burned with fire and the gates consumed with fire. The testimony of God lies in waste, and the people live in reproach. The young have been taken off to Babylon. Why shouldn't I be sad?" All the time something was burning in Nehemiah's heart, he was thinking about something he wanted to do. Wild thing! All Jerusalem had lost her walls. All those of Jerusalem had lost their sons. Consequently, burning in Nehemiah's soul was this: "I would like to go back and build those walls and hang those gates." One man!

Finally, when the king said, "Well, what do you request of me?" Nehemiah said, "I would like to go back and rebuild those walls, hang those gates, and restore the testimony of God." Thank God for somebody who wants to raise up something for the glory of God! Nehemiah wanted to do it!

Hence, it pleased the king to send Nehemiah. So the king sent him on his way. The second chapter of Nehemiah says he arose in the middle of the night, "I and some few men with me, neither told I any man what my God had put in my heart to do at Jerusalem." He would not even dare tell the men what he was setting out to do. All Nehemiah had was a burning desire! A desire to do something. Now, he had it made! He could have said, like most Baptists would have said, "Well, they lost it; let them get it back. They fumbled the ball; so let them get it. I was minding my own business over here. They lost the walls; let them rebuild them! They lost the gates; let them rebuild them."

He could have said, "I've got it made. My retirement is all caught up. I've got nice clothes. I live in the king's palace. I have a comfortable bed, and I have everything that I could want." However, when the king asked him what he wanted to do, he said, "I want to go back and rebuild the walls!"

The king said, "Do you want to leave this comfortable nest? Do you want to leave all these benefits, just to go back and do

something for God?" Nehemiah said, "Yes, that is what I want
to do!"

The Bible says that in the middle of the night Nehemiah got
on his beast and took off with nothing more than a burning desire
to do something for God. But it took more than that desire and
riding out in the middle of the night with hopes high of doing
something for God to get the job done. When he got there, his
desire was tested.

For instance, Sanballat came and tried to talk the men out of
it, tried to make fun of them. Some of the fellows came to
Nehemiah and said, "Nehemiah, this crowd's getting pretty
serious over here. Looks like they are really causing some trouble.
What do you think we ought to do?"

Nehemiah said, "I think we ought to go on anyway. Don't pay
them any attention; just go on anyway."

They got busy. After awhile a messenger came and said,
"Nehemiah, this crowd is getting real serious about this. It looks
like they are going to take up some arms. It looks like they are, by
force, going to try to stop us from doing this thing. What do you
think we ought to do?"

Still Nehemiah said, "I think you ought to just hold on to your
hammer and saw and get a sword and put it in one hand and go
on!" "Well, what do you think. . . ?" Nehemiah answered, "I
think we ought to just go on anyway!" And they did. The Bible
says they went on but with a test. And they realized the victory.

The people also began to rebuild the Temple. In verse 11 of
chapter 3 in Ezra, they sang and rejoiced that the foundation of
the Temple was being rebuilt. Oh, they were so happy!! They
were going to build the House of God back again, and they rejoiced in it. However, in verses 4 and 5 of Ezra 4, "Then the people of the land weakened the hands of the people of Judah, and
troubled them in building, And hired counsellors against them,
to frustrate their purpose, all the days of Cyrus king of Persia
. . . ."

When I read that, I said, "O God, many hundreds of years ago
that happened to Ezra; I thought that crowd was all dead; but
the Devil has raised up some of them; and some are in my

church!" "And hired counsellors against them to frustrate and trouble them." I said, "O God, the Devil is raising them up!" The people said, "Ezra, what do you think? Some folks who have joined our church are known troublemakers. What do you think we ought to do?" Ezra said, "I think we ought to just go on anyway. I think we'll just go on with it!" They did, but not without a test. If you get where you are going, if you accomplish and perfect the ministry that Christ has given you, it will not be without a test. Go on. . .

III. IN SPITE OF EVERY TRIAL.

When fiery trials come, you will have to say, "I think I'll go on anyway." I am not talking about ordinary trials, but about fiery trials. There are ordinary trials, and I believe there are fiery trials. First Peter, chapter four, says, "Beloved, think it not strange concerning the fiery trial which is to try you. . . ."

We would have to say that Job's trials were not average, not ordinary, but were fiery trials. So many times Job said, "I think I'll just go on anyway."

Turn with me to Job, chapter 1. Job was a man who loved God. The Bible says "he eschewed evil." He was a man who worshiped, a man who served God, a man who tried to put God first. But he did not do it without fiery trials. In chapter 1 we read:

"There was a day when his sons and his daughters were eating and drinking wine in their eldest brother's house: And there came a messenger unto Job, and said, The oxen were plowing, and the asses feeding beside them: And the Sabeans fell upon them, and took them away; yea, they have slain the servants with the edge of the sword; and I only am escaped alone to tell thee."

This messenger said, "Job, do you hear what I'm saying? The oxen were plowing, and this crowd came down and slew everybody, and I only escaped. All are dead and all the oxen are gone. We've lost it all. What shall we do?"

Job's wife nudged him and said, "What about it, Job?"

Job said, "Well, we'll just go on and serve the Lord. I mean we'll just go on anyway. We won't quit because we lost the oxen."

Before he could finish telling his story, another fellow ran in and said, "The fire of God has fallen from heaven." He lied! It was not God who sent the fire down. You better watch out how you say, "God took my baby!" Or, "God took my home!" "God took this!" Watch out! The biggest bunch of liars are the Devil's emissaries, the Devil's messengers. He probably told what he knew or what he thought it was. He said, "The fire of God has fallen from heaven, and hath burned up the sheep, and the servants, and consumed them. Everything is burned up. All the sheep are gone. Everybody is gone. I'm the only one that came out alive."

Job's wife said, "What about this, Job? What about this?" Job answered, "Well, we'll just keep on serving the Lord anyway." And while the messenger was yet speaking, another fellow came in who said, "The Chaldeans came by bands, and fell upon the camels, and carried them all away; they slew all the servants and I'm the only one left."

There were three messengers of bad news standing there, and while the third was yet speaking, another came and said, "Thy sons and daughters were eating and drinking wine at the eldest brother's house: And, behold, there came a great wind from the wilderness, and smote the four corners of the house, and it fell upon the young men, and all your children are dead. I only am escaped to tell thee."

His wife and his miserable friends must have said, "What about it, Job? Where is this God who is so good? Where is this God who is holy? You've prayed and you've gone to church. You've tried to live right. You've tried to win souls. But look here! You've lost your camels, all your oxen, now all your children are dead. Isn't it about time you quit serving God?"

Job said, "No, I think I'll go on. I think I'll just go on anyway."

"You mean to tell me, after God has burned up the camels, after the oxen are gone, after the sheep are gone, after the camels are gone, and after all your children are lying up there in one grave after another—you mean to tell me you're going to keep on believing in this God and serving Him?"

Job said, "That's exactly right. In fact, I'm going to be His slave. I'm going to serve Him and be true to Him even if He kills me."

Ladies and gentlemen, if you want to be true to God, if you would finish your course, it may be through some real fiery trials! Perhaps the Devil will tempt you many times to turn away from God and blame God for the things that God did not do. Job was wiser than that. The Bible says that Job later had sores all over his body, such sores according to Job, chapter 7, that the Bible says, ". . .my flesh is clothed with worms. . . ." He had sores all over his body. He said in verse 4, "When I lie down, I say, When shall I rise, and the night be gone? and I am full of tossings to and fro unto the dawning of the day. My flesh is clothed with worms and clods of dust; my skin is broken, and become loathesome" (7:4,5).

"Job, aren't you ready to quit now? Can't you see that God doesn't love you, that it doesn't pay to go to church, that it doesn't pay to serve God? Don't you see you've been a fool?"

Job, in his weak, loathesome body, said, "Though he slay me, yet will I trust Him. And though worms destroy this body, yet in my flesh shall I see God."

Ladies and gentlemen, that is the kind of Christians we need! We need the kind of believers who will go on, as Job did.

In my discouragement, I have thought to myself, "O God, if Job, with a loathesome skin disease, could say, 'I won't quit, I'll go on, I'll serve God,' forgive me for entertaining the thought of quitting. I think I'll just go on anyway."

Consider briefly the literal fiery trials of Shadrach, Meshach and Abednego. The wicked people must have said to them, "Don't you know that if you don't bow down, you will be thrown into a furnace of fire?" And with confidence the three Hebrews answered, "Our God can take care of us if He wishes, if He sees fit, if it is His will. If He doesn't, that is all right, too. We're going to serve the Lord as we are supposed to do." And they didn't bow down to the idol! They went on anyway. Go on. . .

IV. IN SPITE OF TEARS.

There will be tests. There will be trials. And there will be tears. Through a veil of tears many times you will have to say, "I think I'll go on anyway." If we arrive at the finish line, it will be through a sea of tears.

Our church supports over one-hundred missionaries. During the first term of one of our missionaries in Peru, we received a letter which read, "Pray for us. The entire family has hepatitis and is in the hospital." Another letter came. "Pray for me. I'm in the hospital. My wife and baby have died with infectious hepatitis." The missionary was soon well enough to come home to Chattanooga. I was in Chattanooga at one of the conferences. There I saw this man and said to him, "How are you feeling?"

He answered, "Well, the doctors have released me and in two weeks I'll be ready to think about getting back into mission work."

I asked, "What do you plan to do?"

He said, "I'm going back to Peru, Preacher!"

I said, "You mean to tell me that where you stood and wept and cried over a baby and a wife who were given in the service of God—you mean you're going on, that you are going back?"

He said, "Yes, Sir, I'm going back to Peru to be a missionary."

I thought to myself, *O God, how can I think of quitting? How can I think of giving up?* Many times the tears will come and we will have to say in spite of those tears, "I'll go on anyway." That missionary is in Peru now serving God.

Many things could be said regarding tears that will have to be shed: Tears over the unfaithful. Tears over the fallen soldiers who have been lost in the battle! Tears over the perishing. There will be tears over lost people as you weep and ask God to save them. Tears over needs. Tears over dear friends who have turned against you and do not understand you. In Job 16:20, Job said, "Miserable comforters are you all, you friends."

There are tears to be shed! Many long nights of tears will come, and you will have to say in those tears, "I'll go on anyway. I'll serve God anyway. I won't quit."

A businessman met me in Charlotte, North Carolina, who

said, "Preacher, you don't know me. I heard you preach this message in Savannah, Georgia. I was ready to give up everything and quit. I just wanted to look you up and tell you that on that night I decided I would just go on anyway. I'd go on and live for God, run my business in a Christian manner, witness and live for Christ and go on anyway!"

In a preachers' meeting in Georgia, a preacher came up to me after the meeting and said, "Preacher, I came today to say goodbye to my fellow preachers. I've had so much trouble and problems in my church that I made up my mind to quit. I came to the meeting to tell the fellows that I was quitting. I wanted them to pray for me. I was going back to my church on Sunday and resign. But," he said, "I think I'll just go on anyway. I think I'll just go back and preach and pray and win souls and let God do the rest."

As far as I know he is still at it. Go on anyway in spite of the tears. Go on. . .

V. IN SPITE OF THE TEMPTATIONS.

Tests, trials, tears and temptations! You will be tempted many times. "Satan has desired to sift thee as wheat." The Devil is out to get you and stop you. You'll be tempted to quit.

You'll many times be tempted to quit Christian activities for more lucrative things, to sacrifice and lay aside good Christian principles in order to make gains in this world. That is when you will have to say, "Sir, I'm going to go on with God and serve Him anyway."

Through the greatest illustration of determination that I have ever seen in my life, God taught me a lesson of His blessings and power. Believe it our not, He did it using an illustration of the Scripture which says, 'Go to the ant, thou sluggard, and learn.'

I was in a meeting in Miami, Florida. The pastor and I came to the meeting early for prayer. We came through the back of the church. As we came in through the kitchen area, we noticed ants coming in from the door. A steady stream of ants was going up the side and up on top of the cabinet. We followed them and found where they were headed. The pastor was getting a spray gun to get rid of them. We finally found they were after a deceased roach! This roach probably had passed on earlier in the day. The roach was over on his backside, really dead. His arms were outstretched, his legs were hanging, and his feelers were silent. Some of the ants—not all—were busy. It looked as if they were getting around to doing something. I said, "Preacher, wait a minute! Let's see what these little ants are going to do with this roach." We watched. Pretty soon a couple of them ran up and got hold of a leg. Two or three more ran over and got another leg. Some lined up. They looked well organized; they seemed to know what to do. Some went for the feelers, some for the legs, some for the other parts. They began to hold on. All the time some of these other ants were just running in and out but never seemed to do anything. I didn't pay much attention to the idlers at that time. But this other crowd was busy. I said, "What do you think they're going to do?" The preacher said, "I don't have any idea." But when the ants were in place, they began to turn that roach. Poor fellow! He just began to turn around. I said, "Preacher, I want you to look at that. They're turning that roach; it's un-believable!" It was one of those Florida cockroaches. On a linoleum floor you can hear this kind coming, the kind that you don't hit with a fly swatter but get the broom! I want you to know he was a big roach, and these guys were on this thing, and they were turning him around. I said, "Well, I wonder what they want to turn him around for?" We became interested in what was go-ing on.

Pretty soon, the ants got the roach lined up straight with the wall. The guys on the back started pushing. The guys on the feelers started pulling. The guys on the side started. Here he went, straight across that Formica top, headed straight for the backsplash. I said, "I wonder what they want with him over there?" But, oh, they were pulling and pushing. All of the time this other crowd was busy going in and out. Some were running around. I kept wondering: It looks like a big roach to me; why don't these guys push? I wonder why there aren't more pulling? This did not seem to bother the pushers and the pullers. The roach was going right straight across the Formica top. All of the time these guys were just running around. I paid no attention to them. I should have known they were Baptist ants, but I did not until later! They ran him right straight to the backsplash. Would you believe it? They stood him up. Zap! They walked right up the back of that thing. They stood that boy right straight up against that backsplash.

That was the funniest looking roach I have ever seen in my life! Standing at attention! Straight up! I wondered why they wanted him standing up there. And believe it or not, they started pushing him straight up. I mean they started straight up with him. Boy, those guys on the back were pushing. Those guys on the side were pushing. Those guys on the feelers were pulling. That was the funniest looking thing I've ever seen in my life—that old roach going straight up! Now all this time these other guys are still running around everywhere. I started talking to them. And like Baptist ants, they never listen! I said, "Why don't you fellows help push a little bit and pull? It looks like the load is pretty heavy."

But these busy ants kept pushing and pulling. They carried him all the way to the top. However, they could not get him over. So, they let him go all the way back down. I thought, *How sad!* If they wanted him over there, and they worked that hard to get him there, they ought to get him over. I thought these other fellows ought to help, but they didn't. The ants never dropped him. They held right on to him and went right down to the bottom. Then, they just tightened their grip a little more and started pushing and pulling him back up again.

I said, "Now, listen fellows, they didn't get him up that time. When they get him up to the top, some of you get on in here. Cut out this running in and out everywhere and come on and help!"

By now I knew what God was trying to teach me. I said, "I know you; I could call you by name. You sorry thing you come in and out. You don't stop to push. You don't stop to pull. You don't pray. All you do is run around! Get your hand on there and push!"

They didn't pay me a bit of mind, but just went on running

around all over everywhere. These others got him up to the top, though. While I was fussing with one crowd, the others went about their business. They got that roach all the way to the top. They tried their best to get him over, but they couldn't. They never turned him loose. They just let him back down to the bottom.

I said, "Preacher, they've got to be worn out. I don't think they'll try it again. I hope they do because I want to see them get the victory, especially for this crowd over here." I could hear them saying, "You can't do it without me. I've got my tithe in my pocket, and I know you can't get over the top." But I said, "O Lord, let 'em get up, let 'em get up! O God, show those ants how to get that roach up there! Lord, deal with the ones who won't help. Get on that crowd who won't help." They started pushing and pulling.

I said, "Preacher, do you suppose it just proves to be true Christianity in action? While a handful do the pushing and pulling, most of them do the running in and out. The minority does the soul winning. Preacher, do you suppose, if this holds true, that while these fellows are pushing and pulling and some are running around, that some of them would have the audacity to ride?"

The thought hit me! I've got a bunch of riders. All they do is ride. Boy, they rejoice with every victory, yet they have not paid a penny. They have not prayed any prayers nor won anybody to the Lord. They just ride!

I took off my glasses and cleaned my bifocals good and tuned in on that roach that was going up the backsplash. Boy, they were pushing and they were pulling him and they were getting the job done. I looked up there, and would you believe it! There were four of those rascals sitting up there RIDING! And I called every one of them by name. I said, "You dirty bum, I know you! You low-down, sorry, good-for-nothing! GET OFF OF THERE! If they can get him up to the top and can't get him over, I'm going to push him over." And when they got him up to the top but couldn't get him over, I took my fountain pen, put it under that old roach and flipped him up on top. Boy, those pushers and pullers had a jubilee! Man, you talk about a hoe-down! They had a time! They rejoiced. Those ants that were sitting up there riding were the most amazed fellows you've ever seen in your life! You know what God taught me through that? PUSH and PULL! Keep on at it! Keep on at it! If everybody does not join in, keep on at it! If some want to ride, keep on at it! And when you have pushed all you can push, and when you have pulled all you can pull, remember, there is an eye watching you and a hand to help. He'll put you over the top. You just say through the tears, "I THINK I'LL JUST GO ON ANYWAY!"

CHAPTER 2

The Joy of
the Lord

How to Get It—How to Keep It

One of the great needs today seems to be strength for daily living, how to keep going, how to keep up in your Christian life. Where do we get this strength? From whence does it come? Nehemiah 8:10 is our text:

"Then he said unto them, Go your way, eat the fat, and drink the sweet, and send portions unto them for whom nothing is prepared: for this day is holy unto our Lord: neither be ye sorry; for the joy of the Lord is your strength."

Think of it: "The joy of the Lord is your strength." Now, most of you know about Nehemiah and the story of his life, the king's cup-bearer. He was a believer in a foreign land. When he heard the news of the sad situation in Jerusalem and of the reproach in the land, Nehemiah's heart filled with sadness. He became burdened for the work of God and the city of God.

The king, whom Nehemiah served, noticed the sadness of Nehemiah's face the next morning and inquired of Nehemiah why his countance was so sad. Nehemiah told the king why he felt so sad in heart. The king asked Nehemiah what he wanted to do about it. Nehemiah stated that he would like to go back to Jerusalem and rebuild the walls, swing those gates to the city of God, and bring joy, strength and happiness back to the city again.

Daniel, Meshach, Shadrach and Abednego were four of the young, strong Hebrews who were taken away captive. Like many of the young men taken, these were the future leaders of the city of Jerusalem. This caused the elders of Jerusalem to weep. In addition to weeping over the dead and over the brokenness of their city, the elders were weeping over the loss of their younger men taken away captive. The people were filled with sadness and sorrow, as was Nehemiah.

Thus, Nehemiah went back to Jerusalem with a great burden to rebuild the walls, to replace the city gates, and to take away the reproach of the people. Nehemiah wanted to bring rejoicing to the city again. The first seven chapters of Nehemiah describe his return and work. Nehemiah goes back with a burden, excitement, enthusiasm, and with confidence that God will bless him in the work. And God did bless him. He did rebuild the walls. He did swing the city gates again. As many homes as possible began to get back together. Rejoicing began in the land, and their testimony was restored.

Yet, there was one thing lacking—the Word of God. It is not enough to have buildings. It is not enough to be comfortable. It is not enough to have a testimony. There must be the Word of God.

Nehemiah, chapter 8, verses 1 through 3 describe the return of the people to the Word of God:

"And all the people gathered themselves together as one man into the street that was before the water gate; and they spake unto Ezra the scribe to bring the book of the law of Moses, which the Lord had commanded to Israel.

"And Ezra the priest brought the law before the congregation both of men and women, and all that could hear with understanding, upon the first day of the seventh month.

"And he read therein before the street that was before the water gate from the morning until midday, before the men and the women, and those that could understand; and the ears of all the people were attentive unto the book of the law."

Now, the thing that happened when the book was brought out is that which should happen when the Bible is preached. The people were reminded of their failure. They were confronted with their sins. They were pricked with remorse in their hearts because they recognized that they had failed God. They recognized that the reason they had lost their city, their homes, their sons to the Godless nation Babylon was because they had failed God. They had sinned against God. The bringing out of the Word of God caused them to recognize their failures.

Nehemiah, chapter 8, verse 8, states: "So they read in the book in the law of God distinctly, and gave the sense, and caused them to understand the reading."

When the preaching was made plain for the people to understand, they understood what was right and what was wrong. They understood the way they ought to live. They understood how they had failed to keep the commandments of God. Consequently, the people began to mourn in their hearts. Notice that they taught the people in verse 9: ". . .This day is holy unto the Lord your God; mourn not, nor weep. For all the people wept, when they heard the words of the law."

These people had started weeping as the message was plainly preached. As the Word of God begins to speak to our hearts, revealing our failures, we, too, begin to be broken. People begin to come to the altars and mourn over failures to God.

This is what happened to the children of Israel: "For all the people wept, when they heard the words of the law."

All the people *wept*. Would to God that as we hear the preaching of the Word of God regarding our wrongs, our failures, and our sins, we would never get to the place that we cannot be broken over them. We need to always do as these people did— turn to the Lord in repentance and come to God for forgiveness.

Repentance had come. The people had turned to the Lord as they mourned, wept and sorrowed. Then Ezra and Nehemiah came to the people with encouragement saying: "Go your way, eat the fat, and drink the sweet, and send portions unto them for whom nothing is prepared: for this day is holy unto our Lord: neither be ye sorry; for the joy of the Lord is your strength."

"For the joy of the Lord is your strength." There is joy, there is strength in the Lord. Our strength for living is in the joy of the

Lord in our hearts. True conviction of the Holy Spirit of God is needed, but it is not intended for the sole purpose of setting us to mourning and sorrowing. Yes, God wants us to sorrow and weep over sin; but He also wants us to rejoice in what He has done for us. We are to rejoice in His forgiveness. That joy will be the strength of our Christian living.

When we confess our sins and come to the end of ourselves and our strength, we then can discover the infinite resources that are in Jesus Christ. Man has to become completely broken and realize there is no good thing in himself. He cannot go on his own strength. To do so is to fail. Defeat will come if man goes on in his own energy and strength. But when a man goes in the strength of the Lord, he will succeed. For the joy of the Lord is that strength. As Ezra gives the Word of the Lord, he rejoices.

Before getting to the first point in this message, may I say that we are not to confuse the joy of the Lord with hilarity. The joy of the Lord is not some heavenly innoculation or vaccination that causes a Christian to continually live on "Cloud 9" with laughter the rest of his life. Let us not be confused. Satan, as a roaring lion, goes about seeking whom he may devour. He wants to devour the joy and happiness that you experienced in Jesus Christ when you were saved. Satan is jealous of the happy feelings that you had as you left the altar or place of prayer after getting right with God. Satan is out to plunge you into the Valley of Defeat and into the Valley of Gloom. He will take away the strength of your life, which is the joy of the Lord. Therefore, ladies and gentlemen, the strength of your living against Satan will be the joy of the Lord that only Christ can give day by day.

I. JOY WITH FORGIVENESS

The joy of the Lord comes with forgiveness. How do you get it? How do you keep it? You receive the joy of the Lord as you receive salvation. Psalm 132:16 states: "I will also clothe her priests with salvation: and her saints shall shout aloud for joy."

Turn to Isaiah 61:10 and read: "I will greatly rejoice in the Lord, my soul shall be joyful in my God; for he hath clothed me with the garments of salvation, he hath covered me with the robe

of righteousness, as a bridegroom decketh himself with ornaments, and as a bride adorneth herself with her jewels."

A. Joy comes with forgiveness of sins for salvation. Knowing that your sins have been taken away as far as the east is from
the west, never to be remembered any more, gives joy. There is
no past record. You are clean before God. When you know that
you are saved, the joy bells begin to ring in your heart—or they
should begin to ring.

When the joy bells begin to ring in a person's heart after salva-
tinn, he may laugh, shout and praise God; or he may just sit and
cry. But, brother, when the joy bells begin to ring, something
starts happening.

When you get saved, everything looks different. Everything
looks better, feels better. The bed lays better, the chair fits better, the table looks better. Even the old cat is not as bad as he
used to be! The old hound dog is not nearly as bad as you
thought! Things begin to change after salvation as the joy bells
ring in your heart.

How do you keep the joy of the Lord after you are saved? You
keep on drawing from the well you first dropped your bucket in.
If that well was good enough when you dropped your bucket in,
it's good enough now to keep you going. Jesus said to the woman
at the well, "If you drink of the water that I shall give you, you
shall never thirst again." So keep dropping your bucket into the
same well that you dipped into when you first drank of the water
of salvation.

Isaiah, chapter 12, verse 3, states: "Therefore with joy shall ye
draw water out of the wells of salvation." Some of you just quit
dropping your bucket.

Acts 8 relates a beautiful story of how the Spirit of God spoke
to Philip while he was holding a great revival meeting in
Samaria. The Spirit led him down to a place called Gaza, in the
desert. Philip was obedient unto the Lord. When he got there he
found that God would have him join a caravan that was crossing
the desert. God then led Philip to a particular chariot which carried a lone Ethiopian eunuch. God wanted Philip to witness to
the eunuch. Philip noticed that the man was reading in a book.

"Understandest thou what thou readest?" Philip asked.

"How can I, except some man should guide me?" answered the eunuch who was reading from Isaiah 53.

The Bible says that Philip took the same Scripture and preached unto him Jesus. After the eunuch heard the preaching of the message of Jesus, he was pricked in his heart of his need of a Saviour, was saved, and then wanted to be baptized.

No doubt Philip gave the eunuch some New Testament teaching along with his witness. He told him that this same Jesus had already come, that He had died on the cross and was baptized by the hand of John. He also told him of Jesus' command to preach the Gospel to every creature, baptizing them in the name of the Father, Son and Holy Ghost. Philip could not show him Matthew 28 or Romans 6; he simply gave his testimony and word.

I am glad the eunuch was listening to the Word of God. I feel this way about it: If you can believe one part of the Bible, you ought to believe the rest of it.

Philip told the man that he ought to be baptized. The eunuch said, "You're right. Water is right here. What doth hinder me to be baptized right now?"

I like it when a man gets saved and wants to be baptized right away. Philip baptized the eunuch in the name of the Father, Son and Holy Spirit. When one gets saved, he needs to be baptized. Philip says only this: "If thou believest with all thine heart that Jesus Christ is the Saviour, you can be baptized."

The eunuch said, "I believe that Jesus Christ is the Son of God."

The Scripture then says that Philip took him down into the water and baptized him. Acts, chapter 8, verse 39, brings us to the joy of the Lord: "And when they were come up out of the water, the Spirit of the Lord caught away Philip, that the eunuch saw him no more: and he went on his way rejoicing."

Every man who gets saved goes away with the joy bells ringing in his heart, rejoicing in his salvation.

Joy comes—how? With forgiveness of sins for salvation. Joy is maintained—how? In returning to the source of the supply for salvation. This joy is maintained through service also.

B. Joy comes with forgiveness of sins in service. There is
the joy of His presence and fellowship when you walk in the light
as He is in the light. Fellowship with God gives you joy in your
Christian service. The Bible says in Psalms 16, verse 11: "Thou
wilt shew me the path of life: in thy presence is fulness of joy; at
thy right hand there are pleasures for evermore."

Joy will come in service as you fellowship with the Lord. Unfortunately, Satan's target is to break that fellowship that you
have with God, thereby causing you to lose the joy of your salvation.

Christian, you can't lose your salvation; but you can lose your
joy. Sin robs you of your joy. Sin breaks fellowship with the
Father.

After he had committed the sin that haunted him until the day
he died, the psalmist said, "Lord, restore unto me the joy of thy
salvation." David didn't pray to get saved again, but he prayed
that he might know the joy of his salvation. Satan knows that the
Christian's strength is the joy of the Lord, and Satan wants to
take that joy away.

How does Satan take away that joy? By sin. The Bible says
that "your sins have separated between you and your God."
When you get off into sin, the joy bells fail to ring. On the other
hand, if there is confession of sin and a turning to the Lord, then
those joy bells begin to ring again. Happiness begins to come
again.

Satan wants to get you and me into trouble. Sin leads to
chastisement by God. Satan wants us to get into trouble with the
Heavenly Father because Satan knows we are His children.
Satan knows that "whom the Lord loveth he chasteneth, and
scourgeth every son whom he receiveth."

I don't know about you; but when Daddy had to drag me out
from under the bed to whip me, I never thought of it as a great
occasion. I never recall rejoicing about it and being happy. I can
remember thinking, when I was eight or nine years old, *I've got to
figure some way out of this and get away from here.* I was never
happy or overjoyed when Dad was down on the floor looking under the bed and saying, "Raymond, come out from under there!"
I was as far up under there as I could get—where he couldn't

reach me! He would move the bed, and I would move. He would slide the bed, and I would slide. When he would say, "Come out from under there," coming out didn't look too enticing to me.

I used to think Mama's switches were terrible, but Dad never used anything but a razor strop. He would get that thing in his hand and looking under the bed at me, say, "Come out of there!" I never recall it being a very happy matter to come out from under there.

The Devil would like to lead us into sin and place us in the position of chastisement from the Heavenly Father. Satan would like to rob us of our joy and fellowship with God.

The reason some of you Christians are not happy this morning is that you have allowed Satan to get you in trouble. You have let Satan talk you into fiddling with sin.

Look at Hebrews, chapter 12 and verse 11: "Now no chastening for the present seemeth to be joyous, but grievous: nevertheless afterward it yieldeth the peaceable fruit of righteousness. . . ."

Now, where does joy come from? If you have lost your joy in Christian service, you can get it back again by repenting of your sins and getting right with God. When you do this, the joy bells will begin to ring again. The most unhappy person in the world is the backslidden Christian. God cannot bless a backslidden Christian who has sin in his life. The joy of the Lord comes with forgiveness of sins for salvation and service.

Some of you ought to run, literally run, down this aisle, fall on your face at this altar and confess, "Lord, my joy is gone." Repent of your sins. Some of you are in a spirit of gloom. You have no joy in your service. If you search your heart, you will find sin is at the bottom of it somewhere. Get the sin situation straightened out in the matter of salvation, then the joy bells will begin to ring. Get the sin situation straightened out in the matter of Christian service, and the joy bells will begin to ring again.

II. JOY FROM TRIALS

Then there is another source from which joy comes. This may sound like a paradox, but it is not. Joy comes from trials, from tribulations, from testings as they are met in the Spirit of Christ. Trials are a great source from which we can have joy, and thereby have strength.

A. Keep in mind that the joy of the Lord is independent of circumstances. Thank God for that! Happiness depends on happenings, but the joy of the Lord does not depend upon happenings or circumstances of life. You can have the joy of the Lord, yet be facing the most severe tests, troubles and trials.

Look at Hebrews 12, verse 2: "Looking unto Jesus the author and finisher of our faith; who for the joy that was set before him endured the cross. . . ."

Though the cross of the Lord Jesus Christ was agonizing and painful, yet the Bible says that Jesus endured it for the joy that was before Him. How did the Lord Jesus do it? There was joy in it because it meant that He was pleasing the Father. When we do things that are pleasing to God, we know that when we meet the tests, circumstances and trials of life, there is a well of joy within. Knowing that we have been faithful and have not allowed the problems of life to draw us away from our Christian service, we find a well of joy springing up within us. Knowing there is joy in serving God and being faithful to Him, we continue in our fellowship with Him.

So, one of the ways that joy is maintained is by meeting the tests of life. This is the strength of the Christian life. Most of us view wrongly our trials and sufferings. We see the times of testing as occasions for us to be sad. We bemoan the circumstances; yet Jesus said, "Woe unto you, when all men shall speak well of you!" but "Rejoice when you are persecuted for righteousness sake."

The Bible says in the book of Luke, in chapter 6, verses 22,23:

"Blessed are ye, when men shall hate you, and when they shall separate you from their company, and shall reproach you, and cast out your name as evil, for the Son of man's sake. Rejoice ye in that day, and leap for joy: for, behold, your reward is great in heaven: for in the like manner did their fathers unto the prophets."

God is saying, "Rejoice in that day! Leap for joy, for, behold, your reward is great." When testings and trials come in our Christian life and service, let us not take the occasion to be bitter, to be mournful. They should produce joy, knowing you have been faithful to the Lord. Testings or temptations are always, without exception, woven into the Christian life. In every great Christian's life, you will find woven in between the years of work and labor God has allowed certain trials, testings, temptations, even sufferings to come. Trials are a part of life. God knows that from trials we become stronger and gain joy as we meet those occasions in Him.

Keep in mind that whatever God permits to touch our lives, He will bestow upon us, in us and through us the power to be victorious. Never let us ask why these things come; but let us ask, "Lord, what is this for? What can I learn from this? What are you trying to teach me? What are you trying to show me through these circumstances?"

Keep in mind that the wine of gladness only comes from crushed grapes, not from prunes.

In Acts 5, we have an occasion when the disciples, while following their Master's command to preach the Gospel to every creature, were called on the carpet by the authorities for their preaching. They were beaten for their preaching. They were commanded not to preach or to teach any more in the name of Jesus Christ. Notice their reaction to it. "And they departed from the presence of the council, rejoicing that they were counted worthy to suffer shame for his name" (vs. 41).

Can I get joy out of suffering? Yes! Can I maintain joy? Should my attitude be a good attitude when suffering comes? Yes! There is a joy that comes.

Paul and Silas sang songs at midnight. After they were put in jail for preaching, after they had been beaten, they sang psalms and praises unto God because they would not let Satan steal their joy. The Devil wants to take from you your joy. He wants to put an old sour prune look on your face. He wants to steal the smile of God. He wants to take away your "Amen!" He wants to take away your rejoicing. Satan is out to steal your joy because he knows when he does, he has your strength. And when he gets your strength, you are of no use to God. So face your trials and your troubles and instead of bemoaning them, draw joy from them.

The Bible says in I Peter, chapter 4, verses 12 and 13:

"Beloved, think it not strange concerning the fiery trial which is to try you, as though some strange thing happened unto you: But rejoice, inasmuch as ye are partakers of Christ's sufferings; that, when his glory shall be revealed, ye may be glad also with exceeding joy."

If you partake of His ministry, then you must partake of His sufferings. And when you do, then rejoice that you are partakers with Him. You will be exceedingly joyful and happy when you see Him because you responded with joy when the fiery trials came.

First Peter, chapter 4, verse 14: "If ye be reproached for the name of Christ, happy are ye; for the spirit of glory and of God resteth upon you. . . ."

Rejoice, Christian, if you have to suffer, if you become the target of Satan for your Christian testimony! Be happy that you are walking and living so close to Christ that Satan has to take time to try to shoot you down! Be happy in the Lord about it. Serve Him.

Let us look at trials, tests and afflictions as John tells us in John 3:29: "He that hath the bride is the bridegroom: but the friend of the bridegroom, which standeth and heareth him, rejoiceth greatly because of the bridegroom's voice: this my joy therefore is fulfilled."

There is joy for the Christian.

III. JOY FROM THE WORD

Third, joy not only comes from forgiveness of sins in salvation and forgiveness of sins in service; joy not only comes from facing trials and the troubles and the temptations with the right attitude; but joy also comes from the Word of God.

How are you going to get joy if whether you have strength or not depends upon whether you have the joy of the Lord or not? How do you get joy? How do you keep it? Joy comes from the Word of God.

I wonder if many folks are not sour just because they don't read their Bible? That is not the only way joy comes, and that is not the only way you maintain that joyful look on your face, but it is one of the sources from which you can draw. Joy comes from the Word of God.

Turn with me to John, chapter 17, and let's notice what Jesus said in the Lord's prayer. "And now come I to thee; and these things I speak in the world, that they might have my joy fulfilled in themselves."

The Word of God, the preaching, the teaching of the Lord Jesus Christ was spoken in the world that those who heard might have the joy of the Lord fulfilled in them. If the Word of God is not heard, and if the Word of God is not finding fulfillment in your life, then there will be no joy. If you will stay in the Bible and let the Word of God not only enter in but fulfill its purpose in your life, it will bring you joy. Do you know why there are so many sour Christians? They will not hear the Word of God.

John, chapter 15, verse 11, reads: "These things have I spoken unto you, that my joy might remain in you, and that your joy might be full." God wants you to be full of joy. The happiest Christian is the one who reads his Bible, believes his Bible, and receives what his Bible has to say. Feasting upon the Word is a continual source of joy unto us.

Jeremiah, chapter 15, verse 16 reads: "Thy words were found, and I did eat them; and thy word was unto me the joy and rejoicing of mine heart. . . ."

I do not see how there can be a merry heart without the Word of God. We need the Word of God. Show me a Christian who has lost his joy and I'll show you a Christian who has lost his Bible. He needs to go find it again in the Word of God.

Notice what is said in Psalm 119 concerning the importance of the Word of God.

Psalm 119:47: "And I will delight myself in thy commandments, which I have loved."

Psalm 119:72: "The law of thy mouth is better unto me than thousands of gold and silver."

Psalm 119:97: "O how I love thy law! it is my meditation all the day."

Psalm 119:103: "How sweet are thy words unto my taste! yea, sweeter than honey to my mouth!"

Find a Christian who has lost his Book and you will find a Christian who has lost his joy. Find a Christian who has lost his joy and you will find a Christian who needs to get back into the Word of God.

IV. JOY FROM PRAYER

Joy comes from prayer. Now you have to have all of these. You can't pray without having forgiveness. You can't pray without reading the Bible. You have to be able to meet the trials and troubles that come into your life with the right attitude and rejoice in them, as God said. Then you must also go to God in prayer.

John, chapter 16, verse 24: "Hitherto have ye asked nothing in my name: ask, and ye shall receive, that your joy may be full."

When God answers prayer, things pick up. Why are some folks so sour looking? They never get a prayer answered. Joy comes from praying. When you've prayed and God answers, that makes the joy bells ring in your heart! Joy comes from getting prayers answered in your life.

V. JOY FROM WORSHIP

We read in Isaiah 35:10: "And the ransomed of the Lord shall return, and come to Zion with songs and everlasting joy upon their heads: they shall obtain joy and gladness, and sorrow and sighing shall flee away."

Joy comes from worship. Have you ever gotten up and not felt like going to church? Have you ever made the old excuse, "There's no use to go today. The way I feel I wouldn't get anything out of it anyway." We try to excuse ourselves from going.

Then have you ever been of the attitude that you won't get much when you get there, but you went anyway and came back rejoicing? When you go, even out of duty, that faithfulness to the Lord gives you a blessing. You go to the house of the Lord and find that sorrow and sighing flee away. You get what you needed to turn your life around.

Oh, don't stay away from the house of God. Come together with your Christian brothers and sisters. The Bible says that joy comes from worship. The psalmist said, "I was glad when they said unto me, Let us go into the house of the Lord."

VI. JOY FROM THE HOLY SPIRIT

Another way joy comes is from the Holy Spirit. Romans 14:17 says: "For the kingdom of God is not meat and drink; but righteousness, and peace, and joy in the Holy Ghost."

The Holy Spirit makes all the difference in your life. The Bible says there is righteousness and peace and joy in the Holy Spirit. A man filled with the Spirit of God is a man who has the joy of the Lord. That is why a missionary can leave a good salary and a place of comfort in the United States and go to the farthermost part of the earth and be happy. He has the joy of the Lord. He has let the Holy Spirit use him and lead him in the way he is to go.

When you allow your life to be subjected not only to the filling of the Holy Spirit but also to His leading and guiding, then your life will become more joyful and happy than it has ever been. I believe we have so many disgruntled and grumpy Christians in churches today because their ministry has no relationship whatsoever to the working of the Holy Spirit. There are folks unhappy, without the joy of the Lord, because they ought to be working in certain areas of Christian service; but they are not. They are determined to be bench-warmers. Friend, you cannot be a bench-warmer and rejoice on your way to Heaven. Brother, you have to get in the fight, get a part of the victory, and come home with the banner.

Galatians 5:22 reads: "But the fruit of the Spirit is. . . joy." Many other attributes go along with it, but how do you get joy? Where does it come from? From the Holy Spirit of God.

VII. JOY FROM SOUL WINNING

In Luke, chapter 15, verse 5, we read: "And when he hath

found it, he layeth it on his shoulders, rejoicing." This Scripture is talking about the one lost sheep out of the hundred. The one was lost, the shepherd found it, and there was rejoicing. The Bible says, "He that goeth forth and weepeth, bearing precious seed, shall doubtless come again with rejoicing." Do you want to have something to rejoice about? Do you want the joy of the Lord? Then go soul winning! Go after people for whom Christ died. Have a part in winning someone to the Lord. There is rejoicing in Heaven. There will be rejoicing in your heart. And there is rejoicing in the heart of that person you led to Jesus Christ.

There are many sad-looking Christians in churches today because they have not had a part in winning somebody. You will rejoice as you take part in soul winning.

"The joy of the Lord is your strength."

CHAPTER 3

Warnings to Sinners

"Son of man, I have made thee a watchman unto the house of Israel: therefore hear the word at my mouth, and give them warning from me. When I say unto the wicked, Thou shalt surely die; and thou givest him not warning, nor speakest to warn the wicked from his wicked way, to save his life; the same wicked man shall die in his iniquity; but his blood will I require at thine hand. Yet if thou warn the wicked, and he turn not from his wickedness, nor from his wicked way, he shall die in his iniquity; but thou hast delivered thy soul."—Ezek. 3:17-19.

And in preaching the Gospel to you, I seek to deliver my soul!

INTRODUCTION

God is giving to the prophet and the congregation, who are the children of Israel, a personal responsibility to God. He is saying now to the people of Israel, "You go warn them. You say unto them that they can live if they turn to Me from their wicked way; but if they do not turn, they shall die in their wickedness and be lost." In addition, He said, "If you do not go and tell them that message, they are going to die anyway and be lost. The only thing is, I will require their blood at your hands. I am going to hold you responsible at the judgment seat of Christ for failing to warn that wicked man to flee from his wicked way. Now, on the other hand, if you preach and warn him and he does not turn, he

will still die in his sin and be lost; but I will not require his blood
at your hands because you will have delivered your soul." And so
he stresses, "Thou shalt surely warn the wicked."

Everywhere you find warnings; you find danger signs,
something telling you of danger. We try in every way we can to
warn people about danger. We put flashing lights at railroad
crossings. We put an "X" there. At railroad crossings we say,
STOP, LOOK, LISTEN, or DANGER. We put fences around
high voltage. We put DANGER there. We put CROSSBONES
and DANGER on bottles. We put special caps on medicine bottles now that are dangerous to those who do not know how to use
them properly. We are told to take certain things with which we
clean our dishes and our homes and put them out of reach of little children.

Everywhere you look there is a sign that says BEWARE,
DANGER, WATCH OUT. And these danger signs are important
to us because they may be the salvation of our own lives as well
as those of our children. They are good. They are important.

But the most important warnings that have ever been given to
man are the warnings that come from God concerning the loss of
a man's soul. A man may surely lose his life at a railroad crossing
if he does not pay attention to the warning signs, but he still has
a soul to go to Heaven or Hell.

A whole family in my church, the Whitehurst family, was
wiped out on one occasion. They were mutes who had joined our
church. The man, his wife and son were saved; and I baptized
them. They came every Sunday and sat in our Deaf Section.
They heard me preach through the sign language. They were
driving down the road in one of the rural areas at a railroad crossing. There was a STOP, LOOK & LISTEN sign there. Mr.
Whitehurst stopped and looked as best he could. Trees on one
side had been allowed to grow and take over so that one could not
see very far down the track. He could not listen because he was
deaf. His sister in the car with him was also a mute. A girl, a boy,
the husband and wife, and a sister in the family—all mutes. Had
they been able to hear, they would have heard the train whistle
blowing and the diesel engine pounding down the track. Mr.

Whitehurst looked, and not seeing anything, he pulled out on the tracks. Then a train hit them, dashing all of them into eternity!

It was the first funeral service I ever had for five people at one time. An unusual service. It was the wish of the rest of the family that the son be buried in the arm of the father. So they both lay together. It was also the wish of the rest of the family that the daughter be buried in the arm of the mother. So they were buried together. The sister was lying there—three caskets strung out half-way across the auditorium. Five bodies lay in those three caskets. That was a tremendous loss! It was a tremendous loss for the family to sustain, but nothing compared to it if that train had sent five people into eternity unprepared to meet God.

You look at every railroad crossing. You pay attention to every "crossbones" and "skull" on medicine bottles. You listen to every one of those signs on those fenced areas that say, DANGER, HIGH VOLTAGE. Yes, most of you do; but many of you pay little attention to the Word of God.

Here in the Bible are the flashing lights, the crossbones, the danger signals. Here are the stops, the looks and the listens. Here is everything that you can think of to save you from going to Hell. The greatest loss you will ever suffer will be the loss of your soul. Man could not sustain a greater loss than that. He can get by, losing his fortune. He can get by, losing his land. He can get by, losing his health. But what a terrible thing it is to try to sustain the loss of a man's soul.

The Bible says, "What shall it profit a man if he gain the whole world and lose his own soul?" "Speak Prophet; give them warning, Prophet; say unto them, Prophet, Preacher. Speak to them; warn them; tell them they shall die in their iniquity unless they come to me." Warning, sinners!

First of all, I would have you to look at:

I. WARNINGS FROM THE SAVIOUR

Turn to the book of Luke, chapter 19 and notice that Jesus said, "The son of man is come to seek and to save that which was lost." This verse means that Jesus came; you are lost; all have sinned and come short of the glory of God. Jesus preached and wept His heart out for lost men. Jesus came to this earth for one reason and that was to warn men, to die for men, and to keep men out of Hell.

Hell is real! I care not what the modern-day philosopher has to say about it. I care not about his archaeological findings, how many skulls he comes up with, what his test tubes in his laboratory show. God is real! And, Hell is real!

It makes no difference what the philosopher says. It makes no difference what the religious philosopher says. It makes no difference what the Jehovah's Witnesses or anybody else says. Jesus preached about Hell. Did you know that? He talked about Hell. And oh, how He preached about Hell the greater part of His ministry! Thus, the Saviour's warnings about Hell.

Jesus knows what Hell is like. In fact, He is the only one to tell us in detail what it is like. The rich man who died gives us some testimony. He said it is a place of suffering and anguish. He said it is a place where one cannot die. He said it is a place where the worm dieth not. He said it is a place of gnashing of teeth day and night. He said it is a place of darkness. But Jesus surely knows what it is like for a man to die and to be lost. So He warned him.

Let's look in Matthew, chapter 7, at the warnings from the Saviour. If you will not hear me, then hear Him.

"Enter ye [a command] *in at the strait gate: for wide is the gate, and broad is the way, that leadeth to destruction, and many there be which go in thereat: Because strait is the gate, and narrow is the way, which leadeth unto life, and few there be that find it."*—Vss. 13,14.

Jesus said the broad way is the way of destruction. Now look at 8:11,12: this same Gospel:

"And I say unto you, That many shall come from the east and west, and shall sit down with Abraham, and Isaac, and Jacob, in the kingdom of heaven. But the children of the kingdom shall be cast out into outer darkness: [that is the kingdom of darkness] *there shall be weeping and gnashing of teeth."*

Jesus also warns in 10:28:

"And fear not them which kill the body, but are not able to kill

the soul: but rather fear him which is able to destroy both soul and body in hell."

That is Gehenna—Hell. You had better fear God and listen to what Jesus has to say. He is the only one who has the power to send to Heaven or Hell. He said to "fear him which has the power to destroy both soul and body." Fear God who has the power to destroy the soul of man. Listen to what the Lord Jesus Christ Himself said in Matthew, chapter 13, verses 41-43:

"The Son of man shall send forth his angels, and they shall gather out of his kingdom all things that offend, and them which do iniquity; And shall cast them into a furnace of fire: there shall be wailing and gnashing of teeth. Then shall the righteous shine forth as the sun in the kingdom of their Father. Who hath ears to hear, let him hear."

Another warning from the Saviour.

Matthew, chapter 18 and verse 8: "Wherefore if thy hand or thy foot offend thee, cut them off, and cast them from thee: it is better for thee to enter into life halt or maimed, rather than having two hands or two feet to be cast into everlasting fire."

God is not saying literally to cut them off. But spiritually He is saying that if your greedy hands, if your uncontrolled feet, if your uncontrolled eyes are going to keep you from getting saved, it would be better that you went through life with your eyes gouged out, better that you never had a hand to touch a greedy thing, better that you did not have a foot to walk on, than to be able to walk in all the pleasures of life, to see everything you want to see, to accumulate all you want to accumulate, then die and go to Hell. That is what God is saying.

What is it that keeps you from being a Christian? Is it that greedy hand? What is it that keeps you from being a Christian? That dancing foot you have on the end of that leg that is going to go back to dust? What is it that keeps you from walking in the paths of righteousness? What is it that keeps those feet from carrying you to Jesus Christ and receiving Him as your personal Saviour? Whatever it is, it would be better not to have any feet to walk on, but be saved. That is what He is talking about.

In Matthew, chapter 25 and verse 41, we have the warnings of
the Saviour: "Then shall he say also unto them on the left hand,
Depart from me, ye cursed, into everlasting fire, prepared for the
devil and his angels." What a place to have to spend eternity!
The Scripture says that when one dies without Christ, he goes to
Hell. He goes to Hell with the worst trash this world has ever
known. I know some folks who are not Christians, but they are
morally clean. They could not stand a slobbering drunk, nor
someone dipping snuff or blowing smoke in their face. Man, they
could not stand a drug addict or other trash of the world. They
keep their houses spotless. They would not live in a dump. But
some of those same people are going to spend eternity in Hell
with the worst trash ever born. They are going to spend eternity
with the world's garbage. Their ear drums will hear the
drunkard, the alcoholic, the addict screaming in the night for a
fix or another drink. The harlot, the whoremonger will cry out—
yes, all the scum of this earth. And you will be in eternity's garbage can with them if you die without Christ.

Thank God it is just the opposite in Heaven! There is
cleanliness and godliness. If you like to be clean, if you like a
clean shirt and a nice suit and a clean place to sleep, then get
saved! Know Jesus as your Saviour. Oh, He said, "Depart ye
cursed into everlasting fire prepared for the devil and his
angels." Then we read in verse 42: "For I was an hungered, and
ye gave me no meat: I was thirsty, and ye gave me no drink."
Then, verse 46: "And these shall go away into everlasting
punishment: but the righteous into life eternal."

Now, it is your choice where you want to go. Oh, choose
rightly!

Do you want to go to Heaven? Then come to Christ. Do you
want to go to Hell? Then follow your own ideas, your own
philosophies. Then listen to that lame brain who tells you,
"Well, God wouldn't send anybody to Hell." Then listen to that
tired, worn-out lame brain of yours which tells you, "Brother, I
think I'm all right. I'm as good as anybody else." You listen to all
that junk. . .and end up in Hell. Jesus said,"I am the way, the
truth, and the life: no man cometh unto the Father, but by me."

I could go on and on to show how Jesus personally, in his messages and teachings, tried to warn men. "Don't do it." "It is not worth the price." "Get saved!" "It is real." "It is everlasting." "They gnash teeth there." "There is everlasting fire there." "It is eternal there" was Jesus' warning over and over. Not only do we have warnings from the Saviour, but there are:

II. WARNINGS FROM THE SCRIPTURE

We could spend a lot of time in the Scripture, the Word of God. God has preserved this Book for many reasons, but I like two of them. The first is that He may show us that there is a way to be saved; second, the awfulness of not being saved.

God preserved this Book for you. He has preserved this Book for our children, for our children's children, our fathers and our forefathers. Here is the Book of the ages, standing on the Rock of Ages, for all time and for all eternity, warning men. If the Word of God can stand, then everything in it can stand. You have the Word of God this morning, the Scripture. And the Bible warns about Hell.

The Bible says in so many places in Psalms that nations that forget God shall be turned into Hell. In Isaiah 33:14, the Bible says, "The sinners in Zion are afraid; fearfulness hath surprised the hypocrites. Who among us shall dwell with the devouring fire? who among us shall dwell with everlasting burnings?"

Every book in the Bible gives warnings. Chapter 14 of Isaiah, verse 9, "Hell from beneath is moved for thee to meet thee at thy coming: it stirreth up the dead for thee, even all the chief ones of the earth; it hath raised up from their thrones all the kings of the nations."

In Isaiah, chapter 5 and in verse 14, we read, "Therefore hell hath enlarged herself, and opened her mouth without measure: and their glory, and their multitude, and their pomp, and he that rejoiceth, shall descend into it."

Psalm 32, verse 10, "Many sorrows shall be to the wicked: but he that trusted in the Lord, mercy shall compass him about."

Psalm 34, verse 16, "The face of the Lord is against them that do evil, to cut off the remembrance of them from the earth."

Warnings from the Scripture.

Not only are there warnings from the Scripture about Hell, but there are:

III. WARNINGS FROM THE SAINTS

A saint is a Christian, one who knows the Lord Jesus Christ as Saviour. A saint is someone who has been sanctified, set apart, into the family of God by the new birth. Saints try to warn people by preaching, by teaching, by tracts, and by many other ways. There are many stories I wish I had time to tell you this morning. But let me close with this. There are also:

IV. WARNINGS FROM SINNERS

Did you know that sinners warn sinners, "Don't go to Hell"? There is not one man who has died and gone to Hell who would not come back and tell you, if he could, "Whatever you do don't come here!" I guarantee that is true.

Turn with me to Luke, chapter 16, in the New Testament and let me show you this passage of Scripture. Here is the rich man who died and went to Hell, and the Bible says, "in hell he lift up his eyes, being in torments." He begged for water but got no water. He got an answer, but he got no response to his request. Verse 24, ". . .for I am tormented in this flame." Notice his request. 'If you can't come to help me, then I pray thee, therefore, father, that thou wouldest send him [the messenger] to my father's house: For I have five brethren; that he may testify unto them, lest they also come to this place of torment.'

There is a sinner begging somebody to go to his house and tell his five brothers about this situation in Hell so they won't land there, too. Warnings from sinners!

Once a young girl, who had gone to a revival meeting, was stirred greatly about being saved. Her family encouraged her to delay the decision to become a Christian. "You're still a young lady. You've got your life ahead of you. You've got to find out what the world has to offer, and you'll never be able to find out if you get saved." Though she felt strongly about getting saved, and she really wanted to be saved, yet her parents discouraged her.

Not too long after that the young girl was taken ill. She had heard the doctor tell the parents, "She can't live much longer." The parents remembering that she had talked about the things of Christ, said this would be a good time to call the preacher. So they asked the sick girl, "Would you like to have the preacher come talk with you?" She now said, "Suddenly—just like that—you want me to turn everything on! How can I do that? How can I just suddenly feel like I felt when God was dealing with me? How can I just turn that on?"

One has to be careful when he says, "I'll get saved when I want to." "I'll turn it on when I get ready." "God, You wait while I sow my wild oats and do my thing and while I work out everything in my mind."

You better be careful how you deal with God. You are not in the driver's seat. This young girl said, "Oh, how I'd love to feel that feeling I felt at church, when I wanted to go and get saved. How I would love to feel like that again!" She said, "I need to be saved." Then she asked her parents this question, "Would you do me a favor? Maybe this will help. I know I'm going to die. Would you go and pick out my casket now and roll it into the room and put it here by my bed, open it and let me look at it? Perhaps that will stir me to where I once was."

Hesitantly, the family did what she asked. They bought the casket, had it delivered, rolled it into the room, up beside her bed. They opened it. The dying girl reached over and felt the softness of it, but she did not feel a thing in her heart. She lay herself across that casket and began to beat on it and cry, "Oh God! I wish I could feel like I felt at one time! Oh, if I could just feel that way again!" But she could not get that feeling she thought she ought to have.

So now this young lady, not yet twenty, asked her mother, "Maybe one other thing will do it. Would you go and pick out my burial gown and bring it to me and let me look at it?" Reluctantly, hesitantly, her request was honored.

The gown was bought and brought to their daughter. She held

it up to herself. She envisioned how she would look lying in that casket. But it prompted no feeling like she thought she ought to have. Now she clutched the gown and cried, "Oh! Oh! Oh! to feel like I once felt!"

And with all the energy that girl had left, she used it in those last moments trying to reach out and get something she had felt at one time. Finally she fell across that casket, clutching the gown; and she went out into eternity, lost without God!

Do you know what that young girl is saying now? "Don't make the mistake I did! Don't make the mistake I did! Get saved. Listen to your heart and mind as God tries to touch you!"

This is the way God works in you! He uses the feelings and the emotions that He gave you when He created you. You do not have to wait for some unusual outside something to happen to let you know that you ought to get saved! You do not have to look for a shot of electricity, nor wait for writing in the sky. God reaches out with His Holy Spirit to touch the feelings and emotions that He gave you when He created you. That old heart that pounds to get saved, those old fingers that reach out and grab the benches, and the whiteness of those knuckles—that is of God!

If you have any desire to get saved, that is of God. The Devil is not in the saving business. He is out to destroy. God wants to save you; and He will save you, if you will trust Him.

CHAPTER 4

Every Man a Fisherman

"And Jesus, walking by the sea of Galilee, saw two brethren, Simon called Peter, and Andrew his brother, casting a net into the sea: for they were fishers. And he saith unto them, Follow me, and I will make you fishers of men. And they straightway left their nets, and followed him. And going on from thence, he saw other two brethren, James the son of Zebedee, and John his brother, in a ship with Zebedee their father, mending their nets; and he called them. And they immediately left the ship and their father, and followed him."—Matt. 4:18-22.

Jesus, I think, made one of the most promising and prosperous statements of His entire ministry when He said, "Come after me, or follow me, and I will make you fishers of men." This promise was made to Simon Peter and Andrew his brother, and it is made to us today.

I trust that the church activities in which we are involved include the thrust of that statement. The purpose of our church work is reaching that soul for whom Jesus Christ died.

There is a reason that the Bible says, "Study to shew thyself approved unto God, a workman that needeth not to be ashamed."

There is a reason the Bible says we ought to pray about all things.

There is a reason the Bible says we should not forsake the assembling of ourselves together.

There is a reason the Bible says we ought to tithe.

There is a reason the Bible says we ought to be filled with the Holy Spirit.

There is a reason that Jesus said, "As my Father hath sent me, even so send I you."

There is a reason Jesus said, "Go out into the highways and hedges, and compel them to come in."

However, none of these things that I have mentioned is an end within itself.

To know or memorize all the Bible is not an end within itself. To spend four hours a day praying for the lost or for missionaries, to spend the entire day in nothing but prayer, is not an end within itself. To read and study the Bible is not an end within itself, nor is going to church faithfully.

To be filled with the Holy Spirit is not an end within itself; although, many today would have us believe that the utopia of the Christian experience is to be filled with the Holy Spirit. But the filling of the Holy Spirit is not an end within itself. Even the languages which the New Testament apostles spoke on the day of Pentecost were not an end within themselves.

What, then, is the end of preaching, Bible study, prayer, going to church, going into the highways and hedges? That soul for whom Jesus Christ died.

If I know all the Bible and I fail to touch people for whom Christ died, I have failed in my Christian responsibility. If I spend hours in prayer and I am available to reach souls for whom Christ died and do not, then my life has been lived in vain. If I faithfully attend church all my Christian days, never missing a service, yet, my life does not touch another for Jesus Christ, then I have failed in my Christian life. Jesus said this, "Come ye after me, and I will make you to become fishers of men" (Mark 1:17). The greatest promise, the greatest challenge in all the Bible is to touch another soul for whom Christ died.

The most precious thing on the earth today is a soul. Jesus said, "What shall it profit a man if he gain the whole world and lose his own soul?" The greatest thing you can do for God is to bring a soul to the saving knowledge of Jesus Christ. The greatest challenge in life is to be a soul winner. Jesus Christ said to Simon Peter, Andrew, and to us, "Come ye after me, and I will make you to become fishers of men." This is the end; everything else is a means to that end.

Studying the Bible, praying, running buses, having Sunday school classes, preaching, singing—all are means of winning that precious soul. The Bible says, "Jesus came to seek and to save that which was lost."

There was only one reason God sent His beloved Son to this world to die on the cross—that sinners might be saved. Not that we might know more Bible, nor that we might have a church to attend, but that people may be saved.

I trust that this church is different from the average church. I trust that you know what having buses, captains, bus routes, more buildings, and Sunday school space is all about. It is a means to an end. That end is that precious soul for whom Christ died. Winning that sweet teenager, that precious mother, father, grandmother, grandfather, and those individuals in our community that are not saved is our greatest challenge.

And Jesus said, "Come ye after me, and I will make you to become fishers of men." Jesus also said, "As my Father hath sent me, even so send I you." In Acts chapter 1, He said, "Ye shall be my witnesses of these things." He tells us to go into the highways and hedges and compel men to come. In these verses, Jesus gave the first and best plan for winning this world for Jesus Christ. We can't improve on God's plan.

What was God's plan? One person to another person. One individual to another individual. Thank God for television. Thank God for radio. Thank God for tract evangelism. But we can't improve on God's first plan for getting men saved, that is, going out where men are and talking to each one and winning them to Jesus Christ. You can have the largest church, the greatest choir, and the best preaching in all the world but not see people saved unless you go man to man, woman to woman, boy to boy, girl to girl and tell them about Jesus Christ.

Jesus' statement, "Come ye after me, and I will make you to become fishers of men" was not a threat; it was a promise. He was not saying, "Come after me, and I will take off my belt and make you become fishers of men." We know you can't make people go soul winning. People cannot be made to witness. They cannot be made to tell of their love for Jesus Christ. This was not a threat; it was a wonderful, blessed promise.

Jesus said, "Come ye after me, and I will make you to become fishers of men. Men, you are catching fish out of the sea; but if you will follow Me, if you will put your life in My hands, put yourself in the Potter's hand, if you'll give me that lump of clay, I'll make you a fisher of men." Brother, that is the greatest thing that could ever happen to anybody. If there is one thing I want in this life, it is for God to take this lump of clay and make it touch some other life. The greatest experience of being in Heaven outside of seeing the Lord Jesus Christ will be for some boy, some man, some woman to walk up to you and say, "I'm glad you led me to Jesus Christ." "I'm glad you told me about Jesus Christ." "I'm glad you gave me a witness."

I firmly believe that every person ought to be a fisher of men. Jesus said that if you will give Him your life, He will take it and make—not in the sense of force but in the sense of creativeness—something of your life. God is yet waiting for men; God is yet waiting for young people to give their lives to Him, so He can take those lives and make something out of them, so they can touch multitudes for whom Jesus Christ died.

I. COST IS INVOLVED

Now in fishing for men, I want you to notice three things just briefly. First, if you are going to win men to Christ, you have to consider the cost. It is going to cost you something to get people saved. It cost our Heavenly Father His only Begotten Son: "For God so loved the world, that he gave his only begotten Son. . . ." It cost God something.

It cost Jesus something to provide salvation for you. He left Heaven's glory; He came down and took upon Himself the form of man. He submitted Himself into the hands of men. He submitted Himself to the cross of Calvary. He submitted Himself to all of the tragedies and atrocities at the hands of mankind, that he might provide salvation for us. "Greater love hath no man than this, that a man lay down his life for his friends." It cost Jesus to save us.

If this church would be fishers of men, it will cost us something. If you as an individual would be a fisher of men, it will also cost you something. You can't go fishing without it costing something.

1. COSTS MONEY: Some of you fellows who are fishermen know it costs to fish. When I first got into the fishing business, it cost me something to buy boats, motors, and tackle. I got my first fishing equipment on a time-payment plan. When I decided to get into the fishing business, all I thought was needed was a pole and something to catch the fish with. But, as I became involved in fishing, I found it to be a pretty expensive sort of thing.

I can remember first getting started. I went down to Western Auto, where I was told they had good fishing equipment. I told the fellow there that I wanted to get into the fishing business.

"Okay, What do you have? What do you need?"

"I don't have anything. I need everything."

He said, "Boy! You've come to the right place! I can fix you right up!" And he did. He fixed me right up.

I said, "What do I need?"

"Well, you have to have a pole first."

I said, "That's good; I'll take one. . .But, I need two; I need one for my wife."

Then he said, "You need a reel that goes on the pole."

"That's fine, I'll take two of those."

Then he asked, "Do you have any line?"

"No, I don't have any."

"Well, you'll have to have that. Do you have any hooks?"

"No."

"Well, you have to have hooks."

"Fine, give me some of those."

He asked, "Do you have any artificial bait? What are you going to fish for?"

"Oh, I'm going out to catch some bass."

"Well, you need some big plugs."

"Yes, I guess I do."

"Let me sell you some plugs." He continued to sell me some of this and some of that. I was enjoying myself, but not thinking about what it was going to cost me.

He said, "Where are you going to put all this stuff? Do you have a tackle box?"

"No, I don't have a tackle box."

"Well, you need one of those."

"Okay, give me one."

"If you catch fish, what are you going to put them in? Do you have a bait well?"

"No," I said.

"You need one of them," he told me.

I said, "Give me one."

He said, "You might need a stringer."

I said, "Give me one of those, too." And I just about bought anything and everything that a fellow might need. I walked by and noticed the nice, pretty motors they had.

He asked, "Do you need a motor?"

"Yes, I don't have one of those either."

So, he sold me a motor. I bought everything else that I could think of that I would need to fish with.

Then I asked, "How much is all of this going to add up to?"

"Oh," he said, "it's not very much."

I said, "You better add it up."

He added it up, and I looked. . .and I said. . ."Could you put this on a time-payment plan?" Some of you don't know what I'm talking about! You pay a little down and pay a little every month. They send you some papers and a little booklet and you tear a thing off.

I got all that equipment together. All the time he was selling me that rod, that reel and those hooks, I was thinking about that bass about so-o-o long. In fact, it was getting bigger and bigger! I was thinking about all those fish my wife and I were going to pull in.

I put all that equipment in the car and, with fear and trembling, went home. When I drove up in my yard, I said to my wife, "I got us all fixed up to go fishing! I've got everything we need!"

"How much did it cost?" She didn't care what I had; she wanted to know the cost.

I said, "It just didn't cost much. You ought to just look at it. Everything is nice."

She asked, "How much did it cost?"

I said, "Well, you know. . .I mean. . .well, just look at this. . . you'll just. . .just think what you can catch with this right here."

She asked, "BUT, HOW MUCH DID IT COST?"

I thought to myself, *Why don't you mind your own business?* I said, "We have to pay very little."

"What do you call little?" she questioned.

I said, "Very little. I got it fixed up."

"HOW MUCH WAS IT?" she persisted.

Finally, I had to confess. I tell you, I almost had to take it all back! You know what I found out? Before I ever wet a hook, before I ever got to the river, I was making installment payments. You know what I was doing? Getting ready to go. I had no guarantee I would catch any fish, but I had made ready to go.

As I stood in my yard, I began to wonder, *I have all this tackle, and I have this motor, but I have nothing to put the motor on.*

"We'll rent a boat," my wife concluded.

I said, "That sounds like a good idea."

But I found that it cost me even more money. When I went to the lake, I had to buy gas and oil for the motor. I found it cost me to get to the lake; it cost me to rent a cabin after I got there. It also cost me to buy a fishing license.

When I got through and looked at the cost involved, it was a gigantic amount to catch that first fish! In fact, I would have to catch a lot of fish—I mean a lot of fish—to even come close to what it cost me to catch that first fish.

Jesus said, "Come ye after me, and I will make you to become fishers of men." We want to go fishing; we want to catch fish, but we don't want it to cost us anything. We willingly pay $500 or $600, sometimes $1,000 for boat and tackle; but when it comes to catching men for whom Jesus died, we don't want to pay the price. Folks do not want to give money or their tithe in order to buy buses and build Sunday school classes to get people saved, but they will spend plenty on a boat to go fishing. Now, that is not consistent.

Ladies and gentlemen, I'm not saying it is wrong to have a boat. I think we ought to enjoy those things. But, our concern should be catching men for Jesus. And I know this: it costs to catch men. We want to add five new buses and five new bus routes this year. We want to increase the number of conversions among our boys and girls, but it will cost us something. If we are willing to pay for a boat, tackle and for a weekend trip, we should be just as willing to pay something to catch some little boy, some little girl, who will die and go to Hell if we do not reach him or her with the Gospel.

When it comes to catching men for Jesus, there should be no limit on what it costs to get the job done. I willingly pay it, and I enjoy it. It costs to buy radio time, buses, tracts, gas, etc., to get people saved.

2. COSTS TIME: Just as it costs money to catch fish, just so it costs time. The same is true about getting people saved—it costs time.

I fished a great deal with one fellow in Florida. I really was not—and am still not—an expert bass fisherman. I haven't had time to fish for bass in many years. But, when I first went to Florida, this man took me fishing and taught me how to catch bass. This great bass fishermen also taught me that it would take time to get the job done.

One day he said, "I know a place in Lake Okeechobee where we can catch all the bass you want."

"Sounds good to me. I'm ready to go. When do we leave?" I answered.

"About one o'clock in the morning."

I exclaimed, "You mean before daylight! One o'clock. . .in the morning!"

"Yes."

"Good! That's fine with me!"

He said, "We'll stop along the way for something to eat, then drive on down to Okeechobee."

I said, "Man! We'll be there just as the sun starts up, just when we can see where to throw that plug or set that worm and let it flop off that lily pad. . .and jerk it across there."

He said, "We'll be right there."

I said, "Fine."

He advised, "Now the mosquitoes are bad before morning. Get you some 6-12 spray."

"Fine. I'll take a bath in it if it will help." I continued, "One o'clock—good."

I couldn't sleep. Boy! I was dreaming about that big one! Man, I could just see him mounted and hanging on my wall!

One o'clock—I was up and ready to go. We drove all the way down there in the middle of the night. We sat out on that lake with the mosquitoes eating us up, trying to catch that poor fish.

Unfortunately, I have found that people will make a sacrifice to go fishing. But, you tell those same Christians, "I know where they're biting on Thursday night—right down here at the end of Maddox Road. I mean they're really biting. In fact, I was down at that fishing hole a week ago and caught four big ones," and you hear them say, "Well, I don't know if I can make it or not."

Funny how we Christians can get up long before daylight and drive halfway across the county to wet a hook or catch some fish, but to spend two hours out on Thursday night to go soul winning—you never heard so many excuses in all your life. "Well, I don't know; I don't think I can make it."

We are a strange breed, aren't we? We can find time to go hunting; we can find time to go fishing; we can find time to do the other things that we like, but we Christians can't find time to catch men for Jesus Christ.

I've seen good fishermen lay off and lose a day's pay to go fishing. I've seen them lose more than a day's pay just to go where the fish are biting. But you ask that same Christian, "Would you visit two hours?" And you will hear, "I don't know. That would run me in pretty late. I have to get up early in the morning." Excuses! Excuses!

Somehow, we are just not consistent when it comes to trying to catch men for Jesus Christ. Yes, it costs you time to catch men. But God is waiting for some man, some woman, some teenager to get serious enough, to get burdened, to get broken enough for those multitudes out there who have nobody to fish for them—to try to win them to Christ. It costs something to go fishing.

II. DISCOURAGEMENT IS INVOLVED

Discouragement is involved in fishing. If you start a good fishing-for-men program, then is when the Devil really kicks up his heels. He doesn't care how much you pray, how much you preach, how much you sing. But when you start getting active, when you start sending out buses, when people start knocking on doors and trying to get people saved, the Devil gets real interested. I'll be plain with you. There are some discouragements when it comes to fishing for men. Just so, there are some discouragements when fishing for fish.

I suppose there has never been any place where I have gone fishing but that I have always caught what I wanted to catch. However, sometimes I caught fish that I did not want to catch.

I can remember when first I started fishing for red fish. One fisherman in my church said, "I'll go with you. We'll go out to some rocks in a place I know about, and we'll catch some red fish."

Since I had never caught any red fish, I asked, "What do we need?"

He said, "Just bring your tackle; I'll get the bait and everything else."

If you are going fishing for red fish, all night long all you think about is red fish. That's what your heart is set on—catching a big red fish.

We went to the rocks on the water. My fisherman friend said, "Put your bait on your hook." I put the bait on. (We fished with a leader wire on the bottom so it wouldn't get caught on the rocks.) I rigged my tackle with red fish bait. I threw out my line and let it go to the bottom. With red fish on my mind, I sat there for a few minutes, then he said, "Let her sit there; he'll get it. Just a minute. Just be still. He'll get it."

There I sat. In my mind I could just see that fish getting bigger and bigger. Red fish! Man, I was just waiting for it! All of a sudden. . .POW! The fish had struck. That pole went double.

"I got him! I got him!" I exclaimed. The old rod was bending more. I said, "Get over! Get the net! I've got him! I've got him!" And, I pulled the fish up. With surprise, I said, "That's a funny looking thing."

My friend said, "That isn't a red fish."

"Then what is it?"

"That's a big old catfish."

"Is he any good?" I questioned.

"No, get him off."

So, I reached down and YE-O-O-OW!

"Watch out how you grab that thing!" my friend exclaimed, "He has two horns, one on either side and one sticking up on the back. Watch how you grab hold of him. You have to grab him just right."

In pain I sighed, "Oh, man!"

"In fact, you had better use a pair of pliers to get him off," he advised.

"I wasn't fishing for catfish; I was fishing for red fish," I grumbled.

"I know, but you caught a catfish," he said.

"But I didn't want a catfish."

"I know, but you got one. So get him off."

I have been out soul winning, and many times in my ministry I have caught some good ones. But there have been some I wish I had not caught. You have to watch out for them. You can't touch them. Like that old catfish, you have to be so careful how you handle them. If you go at them from this side, they'll stick you. If you go at them from the other side, they'll stick you. If you try to come from the top, they'll stick you. You try to slip up on them from behind, and they are so slick and greasy, they'll just scoot out. You can't get hold of them.

At times I have caught some that have had to be handled with kid gloves. Thorns on them. Horns on them. The ones who were not thorny were so slick you just really couldn't catch them. I have looked back over the past years of preaching and thought, *I wish I had not caught that one.*

But back to the fish story.

My fisherman friend said, "Well, try again. You'll get a good one."

I hoped I wouldn't get any more of that kind. I threw my line into another place hoping this time to snag a red fish. After a while, I got another bite. The pole dipped and moved a little bit. It didn't do as it had done before; this time it bent only a little. Excitedly, I said, "I got one, but he is a little one." Pulling him into the boat, I asked, "What in the world is that?"

"That's a balloon fish."

"Are they good to eat?"

"No, they're not any good."

"A balloon fish," I said. "What do you mean a balloon fish?"

He said, "Lay him down on the bottom of the boat."

I laid him down.

He said, "Thump him on the top."

I did as he said, and the fish swelled up.

"Thump him again." Again, the fish puffed up. The more I thumped that fish, the more blown up it became. Finally, the fish became so puffed up, it was just like a rock.

Have you ever seen that kind of church member? You can't touch them. Every time you do, they blow up. You thump them the wrong way and they blow up. Let them alone long enough and all the air will go out, and they will simmer down. You thump them again, and they'll blow up again. Spotting a puffed-up Christian in the audience, I have looked out and wondered, *Lord, why did I ever catch that one?*

After catching the blow fish instead of my red fish, I said to my fishing partner, "I'm tired of catching this sort of thing. Let me at the other end of the boat." I put some good red fish bait on my line and threw it out. Then I waited and waited and waited and waited. . .and waited. I didn't get anything. Impatiently, I decided to pull it up and check it. As I did, I noticed it had a kind of pull but no fight to it. The rod did not bend; the line did not siing tight, but there had to be something on it. I pulled it up, looked at it, and asked, "What is that?"

"That is a jelly fish."

"A jelly fish?" It just hung there. I said, "I'm getting it."

He said, "No, don't touch that thing! It will sting you."

I lowered the jelly fish down into the boat. . .it was just hanging there. Usually, a jelly fish will slither into the nearest crack or hole when put down.

"Stand him up and let him alone," my friend said.

I answered, "Man, that thing isn't strong enough to stand up. You can't even keep that thing propped up."

I have looked out in my past ministry many times and said, *Lord, I wish I had not caught that one.* Some folks haven't any backbone. You could scoot them through a little tube. They don't stand up for anything. They just run to the nearest crack, slither into it and hide.

After getting rid of the jelly fish, I said to my friend, "I'm about to get tired of this salt-water business. There is nothing biting out here."

He said, "Well, Preacher, next time I go fresh-water fishing, I'll take you. We'll go bass fishing and get some fish." He said, "Now, take that worm—that long black one—and put it on your hook. Throw it right in between that little nook in the rocks and just let it hit the water. After it settles a little bit, then gently pop it a time or two. As you jerk it through the water, something will grab it."

Man, that sounded good! So I threw my line over near the rocks, popped it a time or two, and it looked like the bottom came out of there. I said, "Man, I've got something now!" The line just sang! I was fighting from one end of the boat to the other. The pole was bending. . .Talk about a fight! I said, "You had better get the net. I think he'll break my line."

"Nope," he said, "don't fight him. Take it easy. Get what you can and work him in."

I worked the fish in real close, got the net, scooped him up, and threw him down on the floor of the boat.

My friend looked real disappointed. I was jumping up and down shouting, "I got him! I got him!"

"Preacher," he drawled, "you don't have much."

"What do you mean? He's a good one!" I exclaimed.

"No," he said, "that's a mud fish. He'll bite. Get the pliers and get him off. That kind of fish just lies around in mud and stirs up the water."

Oh, it wasn't too many months ago that I looked out in my church and saw an old mud fish. It seems that all he wanted to do was to stir up the water and keep it muddy, I thought.

You know the kind of mud fish that calls one up on Monday morning and says, "Now, Sister, this isn't gossip; but I just wanted you to know. . .Have you heard?" If that isn't gossip, I don't know what is. "I don't want you to think I am gossiping about the pastor, but did you hear. . . ?" "I'm not gossiping about Brother Morton, but did you know?. . ." Mud fish. There have been lots of times that I have gone fishing and caught a mud fish and said, *Oh, I wish I had not caught him.*

There is discouragement in soul winning and fishing for men. Not every soul you catch on Sunday morning and Sunday night or Thursday night will be pleasing, but these are souls for whom Christ died. There are some discouragements in witnessing and soul winning.

III. ENCOURAGEMENT IS INVOLVED

Finally, let me close quickly with this. Cost is involved. Discouragement is involved. But encouragement is also involved. Not all that you catch will be bad. Not all that you catch will be mud fish, balloon fish, or the kind you wish you had not caught. Catching some good ones is the one thing that keeps you going back.

Once in a while you will catch a salmon that just goes upstream. I mean, the salmon goes upstream and keeps on going because of its determination. You'll catch other good ones, too. There is a reward involved in fishing for men. Sometimes you will catch folks, and you will look back over their lives and thank God that you caught that one.

I can remember many years ago, now, some folks called me. "Would you mind visiting this lady? She is not a very good woman, but she needs to be saved. Would you go and try to win this woman to Jesus?"

I went. The lady looked like anything but a good prospect to win to Christ. I witnessed to her, and she bowed her head and accepted Christ. She didn't have on very appropriate clothes for the occasion. She didn't have very good clothes for the beginning of her early Christian life, but she found some and came to church and took a stand for Jesus Christ. This was nearly twelve years ago; and she is still at it, still going. She was one of the most faithful, dedicated, tithing, soul-winning women that I had in my church. Thank God for the good ones that we catch! Thank God for the good ones we can get if we keep on going.

You want some good people in your church? Then go out and win some. You want your church to grow? Then go out and win someone to Christ. You want your budget to increase? Then go out and catch somebody with a coin in his mouth. Be like Jesus, who said to Simon Peter, "Go down and cast a hook into the water and catch a fish. Thou shalt find a piece of money in his mouth. Take that and pay your taxes."

The best way to increase your Sunday school attendance is through soul winning.

The first secret to success in any church is soul winning. Instead of complaining about your church budget go out and knock on doors and win people to Jesus Christ and teach them the joy and blessing of tithing and giving to God's work. Committee meetings, conferences, and talks do very little. But, Christians going out every day of the week fishing for men, trying to catch people for Jesus Christ, is what builds churches. . .and Christians.

Thank God for the good ones you catch. Jesus said, "Come ye after me, and I will make you to become fishers of men." Jesus can make the difference when you obey Him. I have looked out over my congregation and thought many times, *Thank God, I caught him!* Right now one of my preacher boys—a young man up near Washington, D.C.—is doing a great soul-winning and missionary work. This is the result of our knocking on doors— just fishing. We caught that man for Jesus Christ. Glen Moorman walked down the aisle and said, "I'm here to trust Jesus. I'm here to be saved, to be baptized and to follow Him." Glen Moorman is one who has been going upstream from that day to this. And everytime I see him I want to say, *Thank God, I caught him!*

That young man took a bus route and built it up. He surrendered to preach the Gospel. Going away to Tennessee Temple Schools, he graduated and is now pastor of a good church and doing a great job for Jesus Christ. Since I have been pastor of this church, Glen has called me to say, "Pastor, I'm praying for you. I'm glad you are doing a good work for God. Just wanted you to know we love you and are still praying for you."

Another man called me from New York City, one of our preacher boys from our former church. He said, "Preacher, I want you to know that we are praying for you. We love you and are praying for your church and your people at Pinecrest." I said, *Thank God, I caught that one!*

Yes, there is a lot of discouragement in soul winning; but there is much encouragement, also. After a quarter of century of preaching, I look back and at times have said, *I wish I had not caught that one because he did not turn out to be a credit to the cause of Christ.* But, I can look at the multitudes and say, *Thank God, I caught them!*

Jesus said, "I'll make you to become a fisher of men." I'd rather be a good soul winner than a good preacher. I'd rather my life touch another for Jesus Christ. Since being pastor of this church, I have prayed that God will give me souls in this place, that He would give me power to catch men and women for Christ.

If you want to affect your church, if you want to help Pinecrest Baptist Church, if you really want to contribute something to the ministry of this church, then tell Jesus: "Here is my life; make me a soul winner. Lord, I give it to You. I may not be much; I don't think I am much, but take and use me."

God took a man from the seat of customs. He also took fishermen who knew nothing about fishing for men and made great preachers and soul winners out of them. The greatest height to which any Christian can climb is down on his knees asking somebody else to accept Jesus Christ as Saviour.

There are many ways that you can help win souls. Those whom

you may not be able to win, you can bring to church. You can invite others. You can encourage them. You can press them to come to church and hear the Gospel. You can, during the entire sermon, pray, "O God, O Holy Spirit, take the Word of God and use it to pierce that heart. Lord, bring that friend or that loved one to Jesus Christ." You can be a soul winner in the pew.

The Bible says, "He that winneth souls is wise. . . ." Another verse states, "They that be wise shall shine as the brightness of the firmament. . .forever." Do you know what the real brightness of Heaven is going to be? It will be Jesus, but it also will be the soul winner.

You may say, "But, Preacher, I don't know how to win a soul to Jesus." Jesus will help you. As He hath said, "Come ye after me and I *will make* you to become fishers of men." He will create in you what is needed to be a soul winner. Jesus will make you into the soul winner He wants you to be.

The rewards and encouragements that you will receive for being a fisher of men far outweigh any cost or discouragement involved.

Give yourself to Him; Jesus will do the rest.

CHAPTER 5

Sources to Success

I want to share with you the message from II Corinthians, chapter 5, verse 14. We will use that as the last text before getting to the message this morning.

I speak to you on successful Christian living. What are the sources to a successful Christian life? Why is it that some progress while others regress? While some go forward, others stand still. Some stay in the fight, while others give up the fight. Some raise high the banner and keep it high, while others lower the banner. Let's look at some Bible examples.

First, there was a man named Stephen, found in Acts, chapter 7. Stephen was one of the first deacons. He was one of the first ordained men in the New Testament. He was a very faithful and dedicated man even before his ordination. Ordination does not make a man faithful, but he ought to stay faithful because he is ordained. He ought to stay right, stay straight, stay in the fight and keep going for the Lord. Such a man was Stephen, that great Christian.

The hostility toward Christianity was growing by leaps and bounds, especially under the leadership of a man called Saul of Tarsus who later was saved while on the road to Damascus. He turned out to be a great servant of the Lord Jesus. We know him in the Bible as Paul the apostle.

When Christians were being put to death, were being severely punished and deprived of privileges, this deacon, Stephen, was standing forth in the midst of this hostility and giving his testimony of Jesus Christ. Jesus had already been crucified. At this point in the Scripture, He had already ascended and was seated at the right hand of the Father in Heaven. But Stephen was giving witness to Jesus Christ. And as a result of it, his life was taken. The threats and the danger of losing his life did not alter his stand, neither did it alter his Christian living. Nothing should alter our Christian living or Christian ministry.

So, in Acts, chapter 7, Stephen is standing, speaking to some of the hostile crowd who had crucified the Lord Jesus. Some of them already had been saved at Pentecost. Peter had preached and three thousand at one time came to Christ. But there was still a lot of hostility, as we will see in chapter 7. The Bible says in verses 48 through 60:

"Howbeit the most High dwelleth not in temples made with hands; as saith the prophet, Heaven is my throne, and earth is my footstool: what house will ye build me? saith the Lord: or what is the place of my rest? Hath not my hand made all these things? Ye stiffnecked and uncircumcised in heart and ears, ye do always resist the Holy Ghost: as your fathers did, so do ye. Which of the prophets have not your fathers persecuted? and they have slain them which shewed before of the coming of the Just One; of whom ye have been now the betrayers and murderers: Who have received the law by the disposition of angels, and have not kept it. When they heard these things, they were cut to the heart, and they gnashed on him with their teeth. But he, being full of the Holy Ghost, looked up stedfastly into heaven, and saw the glory of God, and Jesus standing on the right hand of God, And said, Behold, I see the heavens opened, and the Son of man standing on the right hand of God. Then they cried out with a loud voice, and stopped their ears, and ran upon him with one accord, And cast him out of the city, and stoned him: and the witnesses laid down their clothes at a young man's feet, whose name was Saul. And they stoned Stephen, calling upon God, and saying, Lord Jesus, receive my spirit. And he kneeled down, and cried with a loud voice, Lord, lay not this sin to their charge. And when he had said this, he fell asleep."

Here was a man, a Christian in the fight, faithful to the Lord, a man who died rather than give in, rather than give up, rather than retreat. He sat his face steadfastly toward Christ. He faced his Christian living and responsibility even in death.

There is another Christian servant the Bible talks about in the book of Colossians. Here is a man who is just the opposite of Stephen. Instead of having a steadfast faith and staying true to Christ and the things of God, he turns and goes the other way. In Colossians, chapter 4, verse 14: "Luke, the beloved physician, and Demas, greet you."

Look at Demas for a moment. Demas worked with Paul the apostle and with Luke, the physician who was so closely related with the ministry of the Apostle Paul. Here was Demas, working with these two great Christians; but look with me over in II Timothy, chapter 4, verses 9 and 10 and see what happened to this Christian servant. Paul, writing to young Timothy, says in verses 9 and 10: "Do thy diligence to come shortly unto me: For Demas hath forsaken me. . . ." And then he gives the reason why Demas had forsaken Paul: ". . .having loved this present world . . . ."

Here is one man by the name of Stephen who, rather than recant or retreat, was willing to pay the supreme price for his loyalty to Jesus Christ; and that price was death. This is the greatest price that a man can pay in Christian service. There is no greater crown to be offered than the martyr's crown. Stephen has gained the martyr's crown.

Demas was in the ministry as much as Stephen was, working with Paul and Luke the physician; but suddenly he drops out of the ministry. He drops out of faithfulness. He turns aside and goes the other way and gives up his Christian living and turns to the world. What is the reason? Why did Demas turn back?

It certainly could not have been the fact that Demas had no one to help him, that he had no one to encourage him. It could not have been that he never had the opportunity to walk with good Christians; for certainly he could not have walked, had fellowship, been to prayer meetings, been on soul winning, been in evangelistic campaigns any more or with any greater people than Luke the physician and the Apostle Paul.

You may walk with the greatest, pray with the greatest, be in the greatest meetings, yet be out of the race tomorrow. Some of you have sat at the feet of great preachers; you have been in great meetings; you have seen God do great things; yet some of you may be out of the race. You haven't set your face and found your faith steadfast in Christian service.

We always wonder why Christians do the things they do, give up the things they give up to serve Christ and live for Him.

Billy Sunday, a successful, promising athlete in the baseball world, turned from a prosperous and famous life in baseball to preaching the Gospel. Why does a man want to give up fame and fortune to preach?

The Jewish evangelist, Hyman Appelman, was a promising attorney who turned aside fame and fortune to preach the unsearchable riches of Jesus Christ. This is puzzling to the world. Why would a man give up the law field or the baseball field to go preach the Gospel of Jesus Christ, and stay with it?

Such could be the question asked of David Livingstone, a physician with opportunities ahead of him. Yet, he gave it all up to live and die in Africa. His heart was cut out and buried in Africa because that was where his life was given. The world has problems explaining that.

Great is the concern over why some keep going and why some fall out. Why will some give up so much to serve Christ, while others, who have so little to give up, quit their service for Christ? Mystery of mysteries is a man like Stanley Tam who has been a millionaire three to five times over, yet has given all of his millions to the cause of Jesus Christ. On the other hand, there are those who have far less to sacrifice, far less to give up, yet they don't last. They quit. One man gives up fame and fortune to serve Christ while another believer, who really does not give up such fame or fortune, quits. He drops out of the race. "Demas hath forsaken me, having loved this present world. . . ."

What is the difference between these two Christians? What is the difference between Demas and Stephen? They were baptized under the same commission. They were saved by the same Gospel—the death, burial and resurrection of Jesus Christ. They both had received the blessed Holy Spirit of God. They both were given equal promises in the Bible. God is no respector of persons. He promised to do for one what He promised to do for the other. All of the promises in the Bible are our promises. We are all saved by the same Gospel, indwelt by the same Holy Spirit, have the same benefits; yet here is one man who stays with it and here is another man who drops out. Why does one drop out? Why have you dropped out?

There could be many reasons why one man, Daniel, will go to the lions' den rather than miss his prayer time. Some will give up prayer meeting for television on Wednesday night. Some will give up prayer meeting for far less than that, and think nothing of it. What is the difference between these two? What is it that causes one to be an overcomer and the other to succumb? What is it that makes one keep on going in spite of all the difficulties that they encounter, all of the obstacles that are in the way, while others throw in the towel?

There are many reasons why folks quit. We shall not take time to deal with that this morning. I don't want to deal with the quitter but with the overcomer. There are more quitters than overcomers. There are many reasons why people quit. Jesus said that they get entangled with the things of the world and their Christian life is choked out. Others, like Demas, love the world. It may be the love of its money, the love of its fame, the love of its pleasure; but having loved the world, some give up God. Others may have hurt feelings or disagreements. Some are just pure lazy and have dropped out of the fight because it is just too much of a struggle. But whatever the reason, some are out of the race, out of the fight.

But our attention is on that one who keeps on keeping on, that one who is saved and stays with his Christian life and stays with his Christian principles, and lets nothing distract him. What is in that type of Christian like Stephen? What is it that makes him go to his death rather than give in? I think it all begins with commitment.

I. MEN OF COMMITMENT

Every successful Christian has been a Christian of commitment. There will be no continuing unless there is commitment. A man who is successful in his business is a man committed to that business. If a marriage is successful, it begins with commitment. Everything begins with commitment.

It began that way with Moses. The Lord spoke to Moses out of the burning bush and asked him to commit himself to be His messenger and His champion, to go in and lead the children of Israel out of Egypt. God could do nothing with Moses until Moses was ready to commit himself.

So it was with Abraham. God had to speak to Abraham and ask him to commit himself. And Abraham, as Moses, committed himself.

Simon Peter was the same way. There is no use in giving instructions until first of all there is commitment. When Jesus spoke to Simon Peter the fisherman, He asked him to commit himself, first of all. Jesus said, "Come after me, and I will make you a fisher of men." "Come after me—" that's commitment. And successful Christian living begins right there.

In the book of Isaiah, God asks, "Whom shall I send, and who will go for us?" Isaiah answered, "Here am I; send me."

Somewhere along the line Stephen had made a commitment to Jesus Christ. He had committed himself to Christ and all that Christ is and the message that He had given him to preach. Because Stephen was committed, he was dedicated.

There will be no dedication until commitment comes. There will be no continuing in your Christian life until there is commitment. Some of you are not committed to living for Jesus Christ. You have never sold out and made a commitment that you are going to live for Jesus.

II. MEN OF CONSTRAINT

Not only must there be commitment, but there must also be constraint.

"For the love of Christ constraineth us; because we thus

judge, that if one died for all, then were all dead: And that he died for all, that they which live should not henceforth live unto themselves, but unto him which died for them, and rose again."—II Cor. 5:14,15.

That's the key right there—constraint. Why was Paul the great Christian that he was? Why was he used the way he was used? A good translation of verse 14 reads like this: The love of Christ overmasters me. Though there would be a struggling within myself to do what I want to do, to quit, to drop out of the race, His love overmasters me. His love overpowers me. So it was a constraining, overmastering love of Jesus Christ that set the course for Paul's life. Is there no constraint in our lives? Paul says in verse 15, of II Corinthians, chapter 5: "And that he died for all, that they which live should not henceforth live unto themselves, but unto him which died for them. . . ."

That should be our course for living. Living for Him, not for ourselves, but for Him. Is there not something within you that seeks to overmaster you—the love of Christ? The love of Christ constrains us. That implies a force contrary to nature and that force is the force of the Holy Spirit that lives within us, that seeks to overmaster us—overmaster our own feelings, our own will, our own directions in life and pressure us to pursue a life for Christ.

Everyone of us has reason to be overmastered by the Master Himself. It took as much of the death of Jesus Christ to save you as it did to save Paul. It took as much of the suffering of Christ to save you as it did to save Paul. Every child of God ought to be overmastered by the love of Jesus Christ. Paul said, "There is one thing I can't fight against, and that is the love of Christ."

III. MEN OF CONVICTION

There has to be commitment, a constraining force within us that keeps us at it, that overmasters us; but there also have to be convictions. Every one who was ever successful for God, every Sunday school teacher, every bus captain, every missionary was a Christian of convictions.

Convictions—about what? A conviction that I'm doing right, that what I'm doing is worthwhile, that what I'm doing is important. If you don't have that conviction, you will be wishy-washy. You will be an on-again, off-again Christian. You won't be worth the powder it would take to blow you up. You have to have a deep, bed-rock, backbone conviction that what you are doing is right. It's right to serve God. It is important to serve God. It is more important than anything else. It is a conviction in your heart and life. And unless you have that, you won't amount to very much.

And yet, we set aside our service for Christ for things nonessential and unprofitable. There must be the conviction that there is honor at stake, a conviction of pride. I don't mean the kind of pride that goes before destruction. I don't mean pride with a haughty spirit. But conviction that the way you are living honors God. Bring honor to God, bring honor to the church and the work of Christ.

Then you need to have the conviction that it was God who called you to live for Him, not the preacher. And if you fail, you fail Him. If you quit, you quit Him. If there is disgrace, you disgrace Him. We ought to have the conviction that our service is for Him.

Then there certainly ought to be other convictions. God never uses a man without convictions. Convictions of cleanliness, godliness, holiness—those types of things which are important in our Christian life.

IV. MEN OF CALVARY

One thing that Paul, one thing that Stephen, one thing that every great missionary, every great teacher, every great preacher had in his life was a good focus on Calvary and what Jesus Christ did on the cross.

Turn with me to I Corinthians 1, verses 17 and 18 and let's read the theme of Paul's life.

"For Christ sent me not to baptize, but to preach the gospel: not with the wisdom of words, lest the cross of Christ should be made of none effect. For the preaching of the cross is to them that perish foolishness; but unto us which are saved it is the power of God."

And I Corinthians 2:2 says, "For I determined not to know anything among you, save Jesus Christ, and him crucified."

That's the message—the cross. Make much of the cross because the world needs to hear it. Keep telling others about the cross because it reminds you of what He did for you.

Mahatma Gandhi asked some missionaries who visited him during a fast to sing a hymn for him. "What hymn?" they inquired. "The hymn that expresses all that is deepest in your faith," he replied. They sang—

> When I survey the wondrous cross,
> On which the Prince of Glory died,
> My richest gain I count but loss,
> And pour contempt on all my pride.
> Were the whole realm of nature mine,
> That were a present far too small;
> Love so amazing, so divine,
> Demands my soul, my life, my all.

Is your name Demas? Demas had forsaken the ministry. Could you say, "No, I'd rather my name be Stephen; I would rather be Shadrach, Meshach, and Abednego; I would rather go to the fiery furnace than bow down to the kings of this world."

If you have dropped out of the race, you need to get back into it.

It is important that we serve God. It is important that we stand firm on our convictions and that we put the Lord first.

The following is a story of a man who paid a great price to remain loyal to his faith in the Lord Jesus Christ.

U. Bor Sing, the heir of the Rajah of Cherra, India, was converted to Christ by a group of Welsh missionaries. He was told of the danger of forfeiting his right to the crown of Cherra after the death of Rham Sing, who then was ruler. Then the time came. The chiefs of the tribes met and unanimously decided that Bor Sing was entitled to succeed Rham Sing, but his Christian profession stood in the way. He was urged by many of his friends to give up his faith in Christ. He was invited to the native council and was told that if he would put aside his Christianity, they would crown him king.

"Put aside my Christian profession!" said Bor Sing. "I can put aside my headdress or my cloak, but as for the covenants I have made with my God, I cannot, for any consideration, put that aside." Another, therefore, was appointed king instead of this man of God who was subjected to persecution and poverty. Through all this Bor Sing remained faithful to Christ.

CHAPTER 6

Living One Day at a Time

"Give us this day our daily bread."—Matt 6:11.

There are many things that our Lord Jesus Christ taught us in the Scriptures we need to know—not everything we want to know, perhaps, but everything we need to know, especially about living. One thing the Lord Jesus taught us about living while He was here in His earthly ministry was to live one day at a time. That is my message this morning, "Living One Day at a Time."

Our Lord taught us to pray in verse 11, "Give us this day our daily bread." *THIS* day, not tomorrow, not the next day, but "give us THIS day our daily bread."

While you and I may plan and look forward to the future, yet we must live only one day at a time. We cannot realize our tomorrows now; we have to live just one day at a time. Thus, the Word of God and the Lord Jesus Christ call upon us to live one day at a time to its fullest and to live it pleasing unto the Lord. Live today! I find that is challenge enough within itself.

If you can just live today for the Lord, if you can just please God today, do everything that you ought to do today, then your living will not have been in vain. If you can live today successfully, then you can take on tomorrow. After tomorrow, then the next day, and so on. Life is lived one day at a time, and as Christians we live one day at a time for the Lord as we commit that day to Him. I am afraid many of us are so taken up with the excitement and plans of our tomorrows that we fail to live for God THIS day! We fail to do the things we ought to do this day.

Many times our plans and preparations for "tomorrow" are good; we commit ourselves to tomorrow by saying: "Tomorrow, I am going to start reading my Bible. Tomorrow, I am going to start living for God. Tomorrow, I will start going to church." Our commitments for tomorrow are good, but what about today? We do not have promise of tomorrow, only now—today. The Bible places emphasis upon our living for the Lord "now," not later. Notice the words "day" and "today" in these verses:

"To day, *if ye will hear his voice, harden not your hearts.*"

". . .*sufficient unto the* day *is the evil thereof.*"

"*I die* daily. *I am crucified with Christ.*"

Now, there are some things we need in living one day at a time.

I. DAILY BREAD

First, we need DAILY bread. In Matthew 6:11 we read, "Give us this day our daily bread." We are to look to God for food and physical needs. I pull this verse out of context to emphasize that God supplies our daily needs. Read on further and note that Jesus speaks of forgiveness and other matters. But He is emphasizing that He is our Supplier, our Sufficiency. Furthermore, it is wonderful to know that there is a God in Heaven who is able and willing to meet our needs.

I hear folks say, "I got what I got by the sweat of my brow." In a sense you may have gotten it that way, but I'd like to think that it was God who gave me the ability to sweat—"perspire" for you city-slickers. I'd like to think that it was God who gave me the strength, who supplied the breath. At the end of a day it is thrilling to know that God actually provided for me. God is in Heaven and He is taking care of me. Then, I can look to Him, not only for my physical needs, but for everything else.

We are to look to the Lord and depend upon Him. The Bible tells us to trust God for our physical bread and needs day by day.

There is also a spiritual application to make regarding daily bread. John 6:35 states: "I am the bread of life; he that cometh to me shall never hunger." Here Jesus is not talking about physical bread but about bread as it typifies His body in the Lord's Supper. For Jesus said, ". . .as often as ye eat this bread, . . .ye do it in remembrance of me. This is my body, which is broken for you" (I Cor. 11:24,25,26).

There is a spiritual feast in the Lord Jesus Christ. It is not the eating of the Lord's Supper that saves us, but the spiritual partaking of the Bread which came down from Heaven, even the Lord Jesus Christ. The partaking of the Lord's Supper reminds us of what Jesus did to bring about this salvation.

Notice in the Old Testament, in Exodus 16:14,15:

"And when the dew that lay was gone up, behold, upon the face of the wilderness there lay a small round thing, as small as the hoar frost on the ground. And when the children of Israel saw it, they said one to another, It is manna: for they wist not what it was. And Moses said unto them, This is the bread which the Lord hath given you to eat."

These verses refer to the physical bread which God provided for the children of Israel each day. This can be compared to the spiritual bread which the Lord provides for Christians each day. First of all, the Jews gathered the manna every day. God did not give a week's supply. He did not give them a forty-year supply. He did not give them a month's supply. He did not even give them a three-day supply. There was only one day out of the week that He gave them a two-day supply, and that was on the day before the Sabbath which was holy. On the sixth day, they could gather up enough for two days and it would not spoil. They were to gather enough for two days because God would not send manna on the Sabbath. But on all the other five days of the week, God gave them manna for that one day. They were to go out every day and gather up the manna because it was a type of the Lord Jesus Christ.

I do not have time to compare that beautiful picture of the manna which came down from Heaven to the coming of the Lord Jesus. Certainly, our Lord came down from Heaven to dwell among us. The Bible says that the manna was white. Certainly, the white speaks of the righteousness of the Lord Jesus Christ. The Bible says that the manna came all the way down to the ground and it lay there like the hoar frost; therefore, it was within reach of everybody. The smallest child and the biggest man, the educated and uneducated—all could get to the manna.

Thank God, salvation is within the reach of everybody! Jesus Christ said that a little child can be saved because salvation is that simple—the manna is on the ground. There is bread for a little child to eat; there is salvation within the reach of everybody and it is free. The manna was free. Thank God, we are saved by grace! Salvation is a gift of God.

Much could be said about the manna, but the emphasis that we want to study is that every day the Israelites had to gather it. If they gathered more than they needed, it would rot. It would immediately have worms in it.

Look at Exodus 16:19, 20: "And Moses said, Let no man leave of it till the morning. Notwithstanding they hearkened not unto Moses; but some of them left of it until the morning, and it bred worms, and stank: and Moses was wroth with them."

Do you know what God wants us to do? He wants us to go to Heaven's bread oven every day! Each day the Israelites were to gather an ample supply for that day. To do otherwise was disobedience.

Let's suppose one of the Israelites said, "I don't feel like getting up every day and getting out, so I'll just go ahead and get enough to last me three or four days." Well, after the first day, the manna would have worms in it.

I am afraid so many Christians' lives have worms. I don't know how to say this, but a lot of Christians need to be "wormed"!

God intends for us to go to Him. He expects us to seek after fresh bread every day! Because we have lived off old wormy and stale bread for so long, it is no wonder our lives are no better for God.

We come to church on Sunday morning, and we think we get enough bread to last all week, and we don't come back until the next Sunday. Some never open their Bibles, never go to their prayer room, never go to Heaven's bread oven, don't seek fresh bread in prayer, Bible study, or in living for God daily. No wonder they are full of worms!

God instructed the people to gather the bread every day. He told them He would rain down fresh manna from Heaven every day. And God saw to it that they never had to eat stale bread. But to have fresh bread, they had to gather manna every day.

In teaching the disciples to pray, Jesus did not tell them to pray, "Give us a ten-year supply so we won't have to worry." Rather, Jesus told them to pray every day for daily bread.

If you have bread to eat today, then thank God for it. And if you have spiritual blessings from God today, then thank Him for that, too. Tomorrow you can go back to Heaven's oven for more fresh bread. I like the smell of fresh bread baking in the oven, but not stale bread with its unpleasant smell.

When you get up in the morning, it is necessary that you seek something fresh from God for that day. Read your Bible, pray, and live for God every day. Don't try to live off last week's blessings. Don't try to live off last year's blessings. O God, we have to have a new blessing today, fresh bread today.

God is willing to give us fresh blessings daily; but we are so lazy, we don't want to gather them. We had rather eat old wormy bread. There is something unpleasant about stale, leftover blessings. However, it is wonderful sitting down at the table and feasting upon the Lord! Oh, He is the satisfying portion! The Bible says that when they gathered the manna, they gathered a satisfying portion! May we pray every day of our lives, "O God, give us daily bread." God wants you to go to Him each day, not a week at a time. I am afraid that our lives are not rich because we do not seek fresh manna each day.

Did you get enough bread this morning? Would you come back and get a little bit more tonight? Would you like to have a little more? I love Sunday morning bread, don't you? But, I like Sunday night bread, too. And the good thing about it is that His bread is fresh all day! You ought to be back in the house of God tonight. You ought to read your Bible today. You ought to pray today. You ought to seek a fresh blessing from God today.

II. DAILY DEDICATION

Second, there ought to be daily dedication. Thank God for that first commitment to God! We must do that. There comes a time in every Christian's life when he has to make the decision as to what kind of life he is going to live.

I recently spoke in a Bible conference to the students of a school. Every time I speak to students, I speak of three things: the power of the will, the power of choice, and the privilege of committing one's life to Christ.

The greatest power that we have is the power of choice, especially to be able to choose to be a Christian. Another important choice that a Christian has is choosing what he wants to be. But the most important choice a Christian has is choosing what kind of Christian he is going to be—whether a mediocre, run-of-the-mill, half-hearted Christian or a dedicated child of God. You must make that decision. You must decide how far you are going in your service to God.

What kind of Christian are you going to be?

It is good when we come to the place of that first and full commitment to God and say, "Lord, with Your help and strength, I am selling out to You. I'm giving all of my life to You. I make a full commitment to live for Jesus Christ." But you have to keep that commitment every day.

However, one does not have to be saved every day. Sometimes I hear folks say, "Man, I've been saved. In fact, I get saved every day." No, you don't. The day you really get saved—that salvation will last all the rest of your days.

But one has to make a recommitment of self to God every day. You can't come to the altar and say, "Lord, here I am; I commit my life; I give it all to you," and expect that commitment to be eternal.

Every morning you must say, "I recommit my life today to live for You." If you live for Him today, then live for Him again tomorrow. Live one day at a time. That's the way God said do it.

"So will I sing praise unto thy name for ever, that I may daily perform my vows."—Ps.61:8.

"And he said to them all, If any man will come after me, let him deny himself, and take up his cross daily, and follow me."— Luke 9:23.

There was a day that I took up preaching—I followed God's call to preach; however, I have to take up the cross of ministry every single day. You know how many days God expects me to live as a preacher? Every day! One day at a time.

There must be daily dedication. This thing of living and serving God is not just a Sunday, one-day-a-week commitment. It is a seven-day-a-week commitment to Christ. Paul said, "I die daily."

"For whosoever will save his life shall lose it: but whosoever will lose his life for my sake, the same shall save it" (Luke 9:24). In other words, a man has to put away his own wishes and desires. "I protest by your rejoicing which I have in Christ Jesus our Lord, I die daily" (I Cor. 15:31).

Paul realized that living for Christ was a daily commitment in his life. Here was the great apostle, the great preacher of the New Testament, saying, "I have to lose my life; I have to recommit myself; I have to die daily, every day."

"For I think that God hath set forth us the apostles last, as it were appointed to death: for we are made a spectacle unto the world, and to angels, and to men. We are fools for Christ's sake, but ye are wise in Christ; we are weak, but ye are strong; ye are honourable, but we are despised. Even unto this present hour we both hunger, and thirst, and are naked, and are buffeted, and have no certain dwellingplace; And labour, working with our own hands: being reviled, we bless; being persecuted, we suffer it: Being defamed, we intreat: we are made as the filth of the world, and are the offscouring of all things unto this day."—I Cor. 4:9-13.

In addition, Paul said in Romans 8:18, "For I reckon that the sufferings of this present time are not worthy to be compared with the glory which shall be revealed in us."

There must be daily bread in our lives, daily dedication. One surrender is not enough. Many Christians have surrendered to teach, but no longer teach. Many preachers have surrendered to preach, but no longer preach. And many Christian workers who have surrendered to serve no longer serve the Lord. Dedication must be a day-by-day surrender.

III. DAILY FORGIVENESS

Third, there must be daily forgiveness. Living one day at a time means that you need forgiveness for your sins. Let's look at Matthew 6:11,12: "Give us this day our daily bread. And forgive us our debts, as we forgive our debtors."

Everyday I need forgiveness. The Bible says, "don't let the sun go down on your wrath." Sin's debts need to be settled up every day. If we allow sin to build up days and weeks on end and remain there, then we will soon find ourselves getting farther and farther away from God until we are no longer in the will of God. We must settle up every day. The sins we commit today, we ought to confess today.

There is another aspect about daily forgiveness that will help you in your living one day at a time; and that is, not only to seek the forgiveness for sins, but to forgive others. In other words, don't let bitterness, wrath and unforgiveness build up between you and fellow Christians. Keep your life fresh and clean. Don't keep malice and hatred in your heart, but get it out daily.

I've known Christians who are backslidden and away from God. Their lives are cold. They have had an old, unforgiving spirit. I do not have time to deal with this thoroughly; but in Matthew chapter 6, Jesus tells a story that teaches daily forgiveness. He said that a fellow came and said to his lord, "Lord, I know this debt is due; but I cannot pay it. Please forgive me." His master forgave him. Then that man turned around, went out and found someone who owed him some money, but would not forgive the debtor who could not pay him. Although he had received forgiveness, he was not forgiving. And the Scripture says that the lord judged the servant severely because of this unforgiving spirit.

IV. DAILY WATCH

Now notice, there must be a daily watch. Look at Matthew 6:13: "And lead us not into temptation, but deliver us from evil: For thine is the kingdom, and the power, and the glory, for ever. Amen."

"Lead us not into temptation" means deliver us out of temptation when it comes. You must set a daily watch on your life. The Devil is after you. It might surprise you to know what some folks are thinking about as they sit here in God's house. The Devil is after you now; he will be after you tomorrow; he will be after you next year. Satan is out to steal from you anything you have that is good—your home, your children, your testimony. He is a roaring lion going about daily seeking whom he may devour. Let's read Psalm 56:2 together: "Mine enemies would daily swallow me up: for they be many that fight against me."

Matthew 6:13 uses the words, "deliver us." Now look at Matthew 6:34 and read that verse also: "Take therefore no thought for the morrow: for the morrow shall take thought for the things of itself. Sufficient unto the day is the evil thereof."

There is plenty of sin out there today and tomorrow to defeat you, so you must set a daily watch on your life. Be on guard and resist the Devil every day.

V. DAILY TRUST

Matthew 6:25 tells us that there must be daily trust! "Therefore I say unto you, Take no thought for your life, what ye shall eat, or what ye shall drink; nor yet for your body, what ye shall put on. Is not the life more than meat, and the body than raiment?"

In this passage Christ goes on to say that He clothes the fowls of the air and the lilies of the field. And just as He clothes them, just so He will clothe and take care of you. There has to be daily trust. We need not panic on the trip from one shore to the other. If Christ is in the boat, He can say to the storm, "Be still," and the storm will be still. You just put your trust in Him as you get into the boat.

Remember that Jesus said to His disciples, "Let's get into this boat and push out from the shore and go to the other side." On their way, they encountered a storm and feared for their lives. They called on the Lord Jesus, and Jesus stood in the midst and said to the storm, "Be still," and it was still.

We have to trust in the Lord daily. Oh, I know that we make a commitment in our Christian life. We say, "Lord, we're going to trust you now." But then the Devil comes along, and our trust begins to waver a bit, and we begin to have second thoughts about trusting Him. We say to ourselves, *Wait a minute! Is the Lord really taking care of me? Is God really meeting my needs? Now is this God? What is the Lord doing here?* When that happens, just keep on trusting God.

Once there was a small boy who sang the song that we sing so much, "Trust and obey, for there's no other way to be happy in Jesus, but to trust and obey." He sang it like this: "Trust and okay, for there's no other way to be happy in Jesus, but to trust and okay." Hey, that's a pretty good translation! Trust in Him and everything will be okay.

One has said, "Trust in self and you're doomed. Trust in your friends and they'll leave you. Trust in wealth and somebody will steal it from you. Trust in your good name and somebody will slander it. But trust in God and you'll never be disappointed—now or never."

Why should I be disturbed when I know that my daily provision is in His hands? Trust in the Lord. Take no thought for tomorrow. Live one day at a time.

As we live for the Lord daily, we need daily bread, forgiveness, dedication, and trust.

CHAPTER 7

Strength of the New Testament Church

I share these spiritual truths from the book of Judges and use Samson as an illustration of the truth implied in chapter 16. The truth given here is of Samson and his encounter with the enemies of God. I pull the story out of context and use it to make an application. This is not doing injustice to Scripture because the thought we apply is certainly found in the entire context of the Bible. Thus, we are simply using this illustration to make application to another great spiritual truth.

This is a church message. One thing every Christian and every church ought to be concerned about is being strong, being above the average, not being ordinary, but being above the ordinary.

Samson was above the average man. This judge God had blessed with great physical strength. He was God's champion, and a tremendous one he was. The enemies of God found that they could do nothing with this champion of great strength. That's the way God wants us to be and the way every individual ought to be. God wants us to be strong so that we are a thorn in the side of the Devil. God wants to make us a conquering force.

The Lord Jesus Christ said to Simon Peter, "I will give unto thee the keys of the kingdom of heaven." He said, "Upon this rock I will build my church; and the gates of hell shall not prevail against it." As the church goes forth, it will be given such great strength that nothing shall prevail against it or the Christian.

Jesus said, "Greater is he that is in you than he that is in the world."

Any way you look at it, the Lord expects the church to be overcoming and powerful. The church should be the greatest and most powerful force in this world. And God expects the individual Christian to be stronger than other individuals—to be stronger and more apt to conquer disappointments, discouragements, troubles, trials—everything which comes his way. God expects the Christian to be stronger than the average person and to be a conquering individual.

Samson was that kind of man. He was unusual and his feats of physical strength as God's champion were out of the ordinary. Samson's strength drove the enemies of God to despair. The Philistines came to the place where they had to figure some way to cut off the source of Samson's strength and power. Getting to the source was smart strategy.

If you want to turn out all the lights, it's easier to cut the line that carried the power to the lights than it is to take time to knock out each light. That's exactly what Satan wanted to do with Samson. The Philistines couldn't handle the power, so they had to try to cut off the power source. If you cut off the power source, there is no strength on the other end of the line.

Thus, the Philistines decided to find a woman who would discover Samson's source of strength. They were curious as to his source of strength to defeat a thousand Philistines at one time with the jawbone of an ass and turn back the enemies of God. Never had they been victorious over him. He was a strong man who could take a lion with his bare hands and rend him into pieces. He was physically a strong man for God. The people of God cheered him on.

In Judges, chapter 16, the Philistines hired Delilah at a great price to find the source of Samson's power. Of course, you know the story. We read in verses 6 and 7:

"And Delilah said to Samson, Tell me, I pray thee, wherein thy great strength lieth, and wherewith thou mightest be bound to afflict thee. And Samson said unto her, If they bind me with

seven green withs that were never dried, then shall I be weak, and be as another man."

Of course he lied. That was not so. He continued to lie about it. Finally, he told her the truth. He told her wherein his great strength lay. In finally telling the truth, he said, "You do this and you will cut the source of my power." The Philistines cut his hair, which was a sign of his obedience and dedication to God. It was not the actual, physical cutting of the hair but that willingness to let it be cut, his willingness to go against his vow and give away the secret of the source of his power—when he succumbed to that sin, then is when he lost his power and strength.

Now the Devil wants to do the very same thing to you, to me and to the church. He knows what makes a church strong. He knows the place, the power-source. He knows your strength.

Beloved, God has mainly one champion in this world today. Looking through the Old Testament, you will find that God used different champions for His cause: men like Gideon and Samson and others. God used different events in the lives of these men, but they were all champions of God.

However, in the New Testament, the church is God's champion. The Lord Jesus Christ has commissioned and commanded His church. There is no way for that church to do what Jesus has commanded apart from unusual, out-of-the-ordinary strength that only He can give. Think about it. God has given instructions to us as individuals and as a church, for the church is His champion, the champion that God is using to effect His plan today. He is not looking to Samson nor to Gideon but to the church.

Strangely enough, the world is looking to the church. It needs the church. We can say, *As the strength of the church, so goes the nation or the world.*

And the Lord has commanded us to do a job that is impossible in our own strength. It is not humanly possible to do what the Lord has commanded and commissioned without the unusual strength He provides. Our Lord knew that, so He said to His church, who had already been given its commissions, commands, and instructions: "You wait, you tarry in Jerusalem till you be endued with the power of God from on High. Then you will be ready to go out and witness for Me in Judaea and Samaria and the uttermost part of the world."

Likewise, you and I have to have an unusual power to do the things He has commanded. What are they? He has commanded us to walk in the enemy's camp. He has commanded us to walk in the domain of the prince of the power of the air and of this world. He has commanded us to do battle with the Devil himself. He has commanded us to battle the forces of Hell for the souls of perishing men who are on their way to Hell. You and I cannot march into the territory of sin, reach the lives of unsaved men and women, and see them saved apart from the unusual, out-of-the-ordinary power that He gives.

Try winning souls, changing lives and homes, affecting the growth of the church in your own human effort. It is impossible. The Devil knows that, too. Therefore, he wants to cut off the source of power of the church.

A fellow told me the other day that his pastor had said his church was getting stronger. It was going to have more influence and power in the neighborhood because the church was building new tennis courts and bowling alleys. Beloved, the strength of the New Testament church is not in the number of bowling alleys nor in the height of its steeple but in obedience to Christ. And the Devil knows that if he can cut the source, he can make us just ordinary, just average.

I don't want to be ordinary. I never have wanted to be just average. That is why I keep at it all the time. I guess that is the reason I keep after you about soul winning. I push you to get 800, 900, and 1,000 in Sunday school. I push you to read your Bibles and pray. Why? Because the Devil will do everything he can to stop us and make us ineffective. I don't want to just be the average Baptist church, do you? Brother, I want to be—and the Lord wants us to be—a living, conquering, victorious church invading Satan's territory, winning souls, baptizing them, growing and going forward. That is the kind the Devil doesn't want us to be. He knows already what makes you strong. He knows how to cut the power source.

I. SEEN IN THE ATTITUDE OF WORSHIP

What is it that makes you strong? A very simple thing—the attitude you have toward worship. That heads the list. If you lose your God-given, Holy Spirit-led, Bible-instructed viewpoint and attitude of worship, the Devil is well on his way to making you average. If he can get you out of church and away from worshiping the Lord as you should, then you will begin to go down. The Devil will tell you, "Well, you've been a faithful Christian. You've been doing good. Now it won't hurt if you lay out of church Sunday morning. It won't hurt if you miss a Sunday night or a Wednesday night service. God knows you love Him. And God knows you still love the Bible. And God knows you care about souls. It won't hurt if you miss a Sunday." IT WILL HURT IF YOU MISS A SUNDAY! Because it means you've allowed something to come between you and the worship of God. Beloved, the worship of God should be first in your life.

If you haven't already done this, there ought to come a time when you walk out into the backyard or front yard and say: "Now, you listen to me, camper. If you think you're going to drag me out into the woods, have me out on some lake, and cause me to miss church, you've got another thought coming."

Of course, the neighbors will probably ask, "What in the world is wrong with him?" You just say, "Mind your own business. I'm talking to this camper. Camper, I've got news for you. I love Jesus and the church; and on Sunday morning, I'm going to be there. And if you think you are going to move out of this yard, I'll shoot your tires off. I'm going to be in my Sunday school class on Sunday morning. I'm going to be in church. If I get to go somewhere some other time, fine! But, don't you dare try to hook on the back of my car on Sunday. I'll take your tongue off!"

When you get your camper straightened out, then you look for that old bird dog. Lay your finger down on the cool nose of that dog and say, "Now you listen to me, old dog. I'm saved. I love Jesus and my church. On Sunday I'm going to be in church. If you think I'm going to get out and follow you around all through these woods and weeds while you stir up a bunch of birds, you've got another thought coming." You set him straight!

Then you ought to go to that boat and say, "Old Evinrude, I dare you to crank up your motor. I dare you to make a run on Sundays."

You ought to let everything you own—the cats, the dogs, the guns, the rods and reels, the golf clubs—know that you are saved, and tell them, "By the grace of God, nothing is going to get me away from my church on Sundays."

Unless you live with that attitude, you are well on the way to being just a plain, average or below-average Christian. I love you tonight. God loves you tonight. God is looking for you in church on Sunday morning. He's looking for you in church on Sunday night, and He's looking for you in church on Wednesday night.

Some of you ought to look at that toe and say, "Let me tell you something, sore toe. If you think you're going to keep me out of the house of God, I have news for you. I'll put a bandaid on you and take you to church anyway."

Quit belly-aching, toe-aching, and determine to worship and serve God.

A man who is right in his attitude of worship is not going to let anything come between him and His God when it comes time to go to the house of God. When you have everything and everybody straightened out, then go to church and serve God. If you don't, then you will be weak like some of these others.

Whatever your church is doing, that is what you ought to be doing. When you got saved and baptized, you joined the church and God put you in it. All your Sundays and Wednesdays and revival times belong to God. Let everybody know that Sunday is God's day and Wednesday is God's day. The Bible says He made the Mondays, the Tuesdays, the Wednesdays, the Thursdays, the Fridays, the Saturdays; and He made the Sundays. And that takes care of it all! Brother, when God has business going on, I should be in it. Amen?

Show me a person who loses the attitude he should have toward the place of God, and I'll show you an average or below-average Christian. You will wind up average or below in your convictions. You will not see anything wrong with a lot of things when you quit going to church. People who don't go to church regularly begin to do a lot of things which God does not approve. You and I should have the right attitude.

Years ago I read a book which came from somewhere down in Florida. It belonged to one of the pastors. He wouldn't give it to me, but he let me read it. It said that a church was closing down in August and September because that was the rainy, hurricane season. God surely wouldn't want any of His saints to get wet and catch pneumonia going to church.

I would hate to serve a God that made me dodge the weather. I would rather belong to a church that believes in a God who can take care of me when I get wet.

Brother, it is important to have your family in church on Sunday and prayer meeting on Wednesday night. Don't let just anything keep you and your family at home. Bring those children and babies to all the church services. If the little fellows get tired and worn-out, let them go to sleep on the pew. You'll never go wrong by raising your children in the house of God. If you don't have time to wash the dishes, leave the dishes. If you don't have time to eat, don't eat. There is nothing in the Bible that says you have to eat before you go to church. Eat after church.

I think you're getting the point. Put God first in your worship. Brother, if you have power over anything, then use that power and authority to put things in their proper place. And God will bless you in that effort. Worship includes singing and giving and praying.

I will say this much. Just coming to church doesn't really mean worship. Some people come to church to do their duty. They sit there like bumps on a log. They look like knots on a log. They serve like knots on a log. Knots don't do anything. They just sit there. "I would, but I'm not prepared. . . ." "I would, but I'm not feeling well. . . ." "I would, but I'm not going to have time. . . ." We ought to have the right attitude toward worship. If the Devil can get you to stay home, he will get you to do something else. He will keep you from church.

II. SEEN IN THE ATTENTION
TO THE WORD

What is it that makes us strong? The Devil knows that not

only attitude of worship, but also the attention that we give to God's Word is the source of our strength. If the Devil gets you away from the Word of God, if he gets you to reading everything else but this precious Book, he is well on the way to cutting the source of your power. Because reading God's Word is where you get your excitement, your joy, your thrills. Here is where you receive instructions for right living. Here is where you get the food that feeds your soul—the milk and meat of the Word of God.

No wonder there are so many weak Christians. They are on the wrong diet. They don't get enough of the Word of God. You can't get too much of the Word of God. You ought to have Christian books, Christian literature. You ought to be reading materials which will help you toward your goal in life—that is, to live for God, to serve Him, and to be what He wants you to be.

How much do you read the Word of God? If the Devil gets you out of this Book, he will succeed in making you weak.

It's funny how easily he can get you away from the Book. You used to carry a Bible to church, didn't you? Remember when you were first saved? The first thing you wanted was a Bible. Right? There are one or two things a new Christian will invariably ask about. One is, "Preacher, I want you to pray for my husband, and my other lost loved ones." Or he will say, "Preacher, where can I get a Bible?" During these years of preaching, many persons who have just been saved don't own a Bible. I led a man to Jesus Christ in the jail a few weeks ago and he said, "Preacher, I don't have a Bible to read."

You used to carry a Bible, didn't you? You used to want the Word of God. Now you have gotten over that. You just take it for granted. If only one reference to Scripture is given, you ought to have your Bible at hand while I preach. One feels more a part of the message, more a part of the service with the Word of God in hand. When you got saved, you immediately got a copy of the Word of God. God didn't say preserve your Bible, either; He said wear it out. "Study to show thyself approved unto God, a workman that needeth not to be ashamed" (II Tim. 2:15).

Get hold of the Word of God. Before Nell and I were saved, a door-to-door salesman from L.B. Price Company sold me a Bible. I don't know how he sold me that Bible. I didn't go to church. I didn't believe in Bibles, didn't believe in preachers. My wife and I listened to preachers every once in awhile. They would get on our radio accidentally, and we would get them off pretty quickly! We never had anything to do with preachers or preaching or anything else. But this L. B. Price door-to-door salesman sold me a Bible on the installment plan.

I bought a Bible, and I didn't believe in Bibles! He was a good salesman! I put it up and never used it until we got saved. I got saved. My wife got saved. The funny thing is that we went hunting that Bible. It was a big Bible; it had everything: pictures, family records, concordance—everything. It was about five inches thick. I thought that was what everybody carried to church. Sunday, I picked up my Bible in both arms and went off to church. When I saw others with little Bibles they could hold in one hand, I thought, *My goodness! They don't have much Bible, do they?* I found out later you don't have to carry one that big. But I wasn't ashamed of that Book; I carried it.

You were that way, too. Every Christian loves the Book. But then you got over it. You never read it, never carry the Book anymore. The closest some Christians get to the Word of God in a week's time is when they pick it up on Sunday morning.

If the Devil gets your church attendance and he gets you away from your Bible, he has you well on the way down. He has made you an average Christian. That is why I say to you members, "Bring your Bibles." I want you to search your Bible with me. It takes a little longer; but when I say, "Let us look together at the Word of God," and you turn the pages and find the passage just as I do, I am trying to teach you. It is a terrible sin to be in a church so long and then not stay in the Bible when you have a preacher who will help you. You will be average if you get away from the Word of God. It will take your strength away.

III. SEEN IN THE ATTIRE OF HOLINESS

Another thing that makes you strong that the Devil wants to take away from you is the attire of holiness. Without this attire, you will be weak.

Attire, as you and I think about it, ordinarily, is our dress or that with which we may be arrayed or garments. We say, "His attire is beautiful." But I'm not talking just about your outer garments. Oh, I could spend some time on this one. Christians ought to have on enough garments. We ought to be different. If you have knobby knees, don't show them. If you have toothpicks for legs like I have, cover up as much of them as you can. Get your attire to fit the frame. The idea today is to buy the smallest garment you can, then try to get into that more than is proper. You can't get 200 pounds into a 100 pound sack, but some try. You have 200 pounds? Then get a 200 pound garment! If you have 100 pounds like me, get a 100 pound bag.

But I did not mean to get on outward attire; I am talking about the attire of holiness. The church of the Lord Jesus Christ ought to be characterized by cleanliness and godliness. Don't you hate to go to a church where cigarette butts are all over the sidewalks? Don't you hate to go to a church where Sunday school teachers and leaders are immoral? Let the world call us old-fashioned, or anything else, as long as the Lord can say, "I'm well-pleased." The Word says we ought to be characterized by holiness and righteousness. The book of Jeremiah, chapter 2 and verse 32 asks, "Can a maid forget her ornaments, or a bride her attire?"

If I were to ask any bride here, who has walked down the aisle, if she remembers her wedding dress, she will tell me in detail what it looked like. Sure. You haven't forgotten that. Can a bride forget her attire? Look at this: ". . .yet my people have forgotten me days without number."

Notice, again, in the book of Isaiah, chapter 61 and verse 10: "I will greatly rejoice in the Lord, my soul shall be joyful in my God; for he hath clothed me with the garments of salvation, he hath covered me with the robe of righteousness, as a bridegroom decketh himself with ornaments, and as a bride adorneth herself with her jewels."

The writer says the bride and bridegroom adorn themselves with jewels and wonderful garments. And, "The Lord hath clothed me with garments of salvation, he hath covered me with the robe of righteousness." We ought to wear that robe since we are the bride of the Lord Jesus Christ. We ought to be arrayed with holiness, righteousness, and cleanliness.

We ought to have a church with deacons and Sunday school teachers who don't drink or smoke, people who stay away from the world, who dress right and live right. Our whole church ought to be like that. That makes us strong. Numbers do not mean strength. A church may have an attendance of 1,500; but if she is characterized by carnal, religious cheapness, there is no strength in her. We are the bride of Christ. We have been espoused to Him.

The book of Revelation, chapter 19, tells us that because we are the bride of Christ, we will sit down with Him at the marriage supper of the Lamb. Look at verses 7 and 8:

"Let us be glad and rejoice, and give honour to him: for the marriage of the Lamb is come, and his wife hath made herself ready. And to her was granted that she should be arrayed in fine linen, clean and white: for the fine linen is the righteousness of saints."

At a wedding the bride doesn't come down to the altar the way she comes down to cook breakfast ten years later. . . . Sometimes it doesn't take that long—two years? The beautiful garments are gone. There is no perfume, no lipstick, no shoes. Sometimes there is no hair! Were she to come down the aisle like that, the bridegroom would be shocked. But, the bride makes herself ready. *"Let us be glad and rejoice, and give honour. . .for the marriage of the Lamb is come, and his wife hath made herself ready."*

You and I are on our way to meet the Bridegroom. Are you what you want to be? or should you be more like you were the day you were saved? You had a beauty about you. You radiated the love of Christ.

These poor women—bless their hearts—no wonder they come down to cook breakfast looking so bad. They wake up and see a bearded, grumpy man. We should be at our best because we are on our way to meet Him. We ought to look our best and be our best. If the Devil gets the attire of our holiness, he has made us weak and average. I don't want to be average.

Let me give you the last two thoughts of this message. The Devil knows what makes a church strong, what keeps it going, and the reason God blesses it.

IV. SEEN IN THE ACTIVITY OF SOUL WINNING

The reason God pours out His Holy Spirit in unusual power upon the church is that the church has the right attitude toward soul winning. God won't pour out His Holy Spirit and fill you just to cut a bunch of monkeyshines. He will fill you with His Holy Spirit for soul winning. That is the reason He sent His Holy Spirit on the day of Pentecost. The disciples could practice what He commanded them to do. What was that? "Go ye into all the world and teach all nations, baptizing them in the name of the Father, and of the Son, and of the Holy Ghost."

That is why He said to wait and tarry at Jerusalem until you be endued with power. A church that does not have the right attitude and is not active in soul winning is weak. If you let the Devil keep you from getting actively involved in winning souls, he has made you weak, though you may not even know it.

Samson is asleep, his hair has been cut, and when Delilah said, "The Philistines are here," Samson jumped up as at other times and went out to meet the Philistines; and the Bible says, "And he wist not that the Lord was departed from him."

Some of you are sleeping and don't even know that your strength is gone. You haven't met any enemies. But the first time you run up against the enemy, you will find that you are weak like anybody else. We must be actively winning souls as were the apostles who went "daily from house to house."

V. SEEN IN OUR ALLEGIANCE TO CHRIST

Last, and I must close with this point. The strength of the New Testament church is seen in its allegiance to Christ. And every child of God should pledge his allegiance to the Son of God who loved us and gave Himself for us.

Allegiance means to be subject to one ruler, or the loyalty and devotion given to one who claims to be the master. I am ashamed of some who call themselves Christians, whose allegiance is so poor. Everything else comes ahead of God. It seems they reserve the right to break any of the commands or laws of God they feel like breaking. That means they have allowed other things or other people to steal away their allegiance to Jesus Christ. Some say, "I don't like the way the church spends money." Therefore, they won't give to God. Others say, "I used to go to church. . ., but, I don't anymore." When they quit, they withdrew their allegiance to Jesus Christ.

I read a story about a band of soldiers who gave their lives in allegiance to Christ rather than accept favor of their Roman Emperor. These were fine, stalwart men, picked from the best and bravest of the land and recruited from the great athletes of the Roman amphitheater. Before each contest, they stood before the Emperor's throne and rang out the cry: "We, the wrestlers, wrestling for thee, O Emperor, to win for thee the victory and from thee the victor's crown!"

News reached the Emperor that many of these men had accepted the Christian faith. To be a Christian meant death, even to those who served Nero best. No soldiers were braver or more loyal than this band of wrestlers.

However, a decree was sent out from Nero by the centurion Vespasian: "If there be any among the soldiers who cling to the faith of the Christians, they must die!"

The decree was received in the dead of winter. The soldiers were camped on the shore of a frozen inland lake. The winter had been bitter and the hardships had been many. It was with sinking heart that Vespasian, the centurion, read the Emperor's message. Yet to a soldier there is one word supreme—"duty."

Vespasian called the soldiers together and asked the question, "Are there any among you who cling to the faith of the Christians? If so, let him step forward!"

Forty wrestlers instantly stepped forward two paces, respectfully saluted, and stood at attention. Vespasian paused. He had not expected so many. Said he, "The decree has come from your Emperor that any who cling to the faith of the Christians must die! For the sake of your country, your comrades, your loved ones, renounce this false faith!" Not one of the forty moved.

"Until sundown, I shall await your answer," said Vespasian. Sundown came. Again the question was asked. Again the forty wrestlers stepped forward and stood at attention.

Vespasian pleaded with them long and earnestly without prevailing upon a single man to deny his Lord. Finally he said, "The decree of the Emperor must be obeyed, but I am not willing that your blood be on your comrades. I am going to order that you march out upon the lake of ice and I shall leave you there to the mercy of the elements. Warm fires, however, will be waiting to welcome any willing to renounce this false faith."

The forty wrestlers were stripped and then without a word, they marched toward the lake of ice. As they marched they broke into chorus: "Forty wrestlers, wrestling for Thee, O Christ, to win for Thee the victory and from Thee, the Victor's crown."

Through the long hours of the night, Vespasian, the centurion, stood by his campfire and waited; and all through the long night there came to him fainter and fainter the wrestlers' song.

As morning drew near, one figure, overcome by exposure, crept quietly toward the fire; in the extremity of his suffering he had renounced his Lord. Faintly but clearly from out of the darkness came the song, "Thirty-nine wrestlers, wrestling for Thee, O Christ, to win for Thee the victory and from Thee, the Victor's crown!"

Vespasian looked at the figure drawing close to the fire—and then out into the darkness whence came the song of faith. Once again he looked—ah, who can say, perhaps he saw the greater light shining there in the darkness! Off came his helmet, his shield, and he sprang upon the ice, crying, "Forty wrestlers, wrestling for Thee, O Christ, to win for Thee the victory and from Thee, the Victor's crown!"

The strength of these wrestlers was their faith and allegiance to Christ.

CHAPTER 8

The Filling of the
Holy Spirit

"Be not drunk with wine, wherein is excess; but be filled with the Spirit."—Eph. 5:18.

One of the most misunderstood, misrepresented and misused messages in Christian circles is that of the Holy Spirit; yet the Bible is very plain and clear concerning this most important message. This is vital to the believer. Now, beloved, take your Bible, and let us follow along together.

There is a failure today to recognize the one person who means the difference between defeat and victory in our lives—the Holy Spirit. We have failed to recognize His personality. We have failed to recognize His presence. We have failed to recognize His purpose. And we have failed to recognize His power.

While we may admit He has a great ministry in leading, guiding, teaching, satisfying, sealing and sustaining us, there is a failure to speak concerning the filling of the Holy Spirit. There is a failure to speak much on this blessed and wonderful doctrine because of the misrepresentation by some groups. In some groups there is a misuse of the great doctrine of the Holy Spirit. On the other hand, there is the unuse by some of the great doctrine of the Holy Spirit. Because His ministry in filling the believer has been so misrepresented, it does not mean that we are to turn from this command in Ephesians 5 to "be filled with the Spirit."

The Baptists have failed to preach the filling of the Holy Spirit, yet this is the vital message of the day. This is the reason for the formality, the coldness, the calmness, the complacency in our churches. Beloved, the one thing that makes the difference is the FILLING of the Holy Spirit of God. The Holy Spirit alone can produce what is needed in our lives and in the lives of our churches, enabling us to be what we are supposed to be for God. We have substituted everything for the filling of the Holy Spirit. My wastepaper basket is full of programs showing us HOW to get the job done. But it is not so much a matter of knowing HOW to get the job done. What we need is the Power to GET THE JOB DONE!

There was no problem with the early church when the people were filled with the Holy Spirit. Read the book of Acts and you will find those people were faithful in their witnessing, in their giving and in other sacrificial work for Jesus Christ. Through the years we have sought to pattern our churches after that church because of the great impression it made upon the world. We need to make the same impression for Jesus Christ upon our generation. This cannot be done in the energy of the flesh.

The Bible says, "Be not drunk with wine, wherein is excess; but be filled with the Spirit." Let me ask you, as a believer, have you ever been filled with the Holy Spirit? I am not preaching a strange doctrine. If it is strange to you, then you have not studied the Bible nor been under sound gospel, Bible preaching, for this is a Bible message. Do you need to be filled with God's Spirit today? You know if there is no POWER to witness and win men to Christ. This POWER comes only through the filling of the Holy Spirit.

I. THE COMMAND FOR THE FILLING

"But ye shall receive power, after that the Holy Ghost is come upon you: and ye shall be witnesses unto me both in Jerusalem, and in all Judaea, and in Samaria, and unto the uttermost part of the earth."—Acts 1:8.

In the first chapter of Acts, you will see that this COMMAND came because there was a need. Verse 7 says, "And he said unto them, It is not for you to know the times or the seasons, which the Father hath put in his own power." Now verse 8: "But ye shall receive power, after that the Holy Ghost is come upon you: and ye shall be witnesses unto me both in Jerusalem, and in all Judaea, and in Samaria, and unto the uttermost part of the earth."

The command to be filled with the Holy Spirit of God came because there was a need in the lives of those early followers of Jesus Christ. Jesus Himself saw the need when He commanded His disciples to "tarry ye in Jerusalem," and the prayer meeting that existed for those ten days was climaxed with the filling of the Holy Spirit.

Beloved, today Jesus says that we, too, need to be filled with the Holy Spirit. If being taught by a Bible teacher were enough, if knowing the Word of God were enough, then these early disciples and followers of Christ were surely qualified to get the job done for Christ; for they had sat at the feet of the Teacher of all teachers—the Son of God Himself.

Even the Scribes and Pharisees said of Him "that he speaks with authority," and they were confounded with what wisdom the Lord spoke. Even in His early life—at twelve years of age— they were amazed with what wisdom the Lord Jesus spoke in the Temple. So if being taught, and if sitting at the feet of great teachers were enough, then surely these early disciples were well qualified men. Yet Jesus said unto them, "Ye need to be filled with the Holy Spirit."

If hearing great preaching were enough to get the job done that God has called us to do, then the early followers of Jesus Christ were well qualified men; for they had not only sat at the feet of the great Teacher; but they had traveled with Him from city to city and had heard the Prince of Preachers—the Son of God. Oh, how He preached! They heard His message. Yet the Lord Jesus said unto them, "Tarry ye in the city of Jerusalem, until ye be endued with power from on high."

If seeing the job done first hand were enough, then these men were well qualified; for as the early followers of the Lord Jesus Christ traveled with Him, they saw Christ put into practice what He taught, what He preached; and they saw the job done before their very eyes. They saw Him when He called Zacchaeus down from the tree and spoke to him. They saw Him as He spoke to blind Bartimaeus. On through the Word of God. . .many incidents are recorded for us in Scripture as to how Christ dealt personally with men. I am persuaded that what He has empowered us for, what He has called us for, is to deal personally with humanity.

If going out firsthand and going in the field on training were enough to get the job done, then surely these men, who went with Christ from city to city, from street to street, from man to man, from woman to woman, were well qualified.

Beloved, I am for personal visitation. I am for taking a new convert and helping that person, teaching that person, showing that person how to become an effective soul winner for Jesus Christ. But, my friends, teaching was not enough, and hearing great preachers was not enough, and seeing the job done personally and visibly was not enough for Christ's early followers. If they needed the filling and the empowering and the anointing of the Holy Spirit of God, certainly you and I also need to be filled with the Holy Spirit. After knowing what it was to be filled with the Holy Spirit, the disciples were aware of their desperate need of the power of the Spirit upon their lives. The Bible tells us in Acts 4: 31 that they prayed to be filled with Holy Spirit: "And when they had prayed, the place was shaken where they were assembled together; and they were all filled with the Holy Ghost, and they spake the word of God with boldness."

Today you and I need filling. We need the same power to get the job done for Christ that the followers had nearly two thousand years ago. The world has not changed; men are still sinners. They may dress differently and travel differently, but they are the same.

If these early followers of Christ needed to be filled with the Holy Spirit in order to get the work done for Christ, then surely you and I must have it.

Now we are not talking about salvation but about that which follows the saving grace of God. I know many Christians who are saved, but they have no power. There is no real testimony for God. They are mediocre and cold and calloused. Yet there are those who are saved and have a mighty testimony and live a powerful life for Christ. If you follow through church history and read about those spiritual giants of yesterday, you will find that they gave testimony of the filling of the Holy Spirit. Take men like D. L. Moody, Charles H. Spurgeon, R. A. Torrey, Wilbur Chapman, Billy Sunday, men who stirred the continents of the world for God, men who had the power of God upon them, men who saw men and women, boys and girls, by the thousands, saved—all gave this testimony. The late Dr. John R. Rice wrote a book which includes the testimonies of these great men of God. In it he shows how, after being saved, they came to realize there was something lacking in their lives, something else they needed—the filling of the Holy Spirit. This is scriptural, because the Bible commands Christians to be filled. The early followers of Christ needed to be filled. And if these great men, who stirred the nations in our past generations for God, saw the need, then surely you and I ought to awaken to the fact that we need it if we are to make an impression on our generation for Jesus Christ. IN ORDER NOT TO FAIL, WE MUST BE FILLED.

Peter realized that he needed something more than he could get from a mid-week or Sunday night meeting, or more than he could get from a few study courses on how to get the job done.

The heartbreak of the hour is that there seems to be no desire for God's power. Now you may take courses on how to get the job done, on how to battle Satan; but you cannot do either without the power of the Spirit of God. How many times have you wished your church was like those in the book of Acts. Well, it won't be, apart from the filling of the Holy Spirit.

Today, if your life is full of failures, full of defeat, then you need to be filled with the Holy Spirit. This does not belong to any particular denomination. This is a simple Bible command to any and all who believe and accept the Bible as the Word of God. This is your command and this is my command: "be filled with the Spirit."

If you have never been saved, then you need to pray and ask God to save you first of all. Jesus is the only way, the cross of Calvary is the only way of salvation. The Bible says that

"whosoever shall call upon the name of the Lord shall be saved."
Will you call upon Him today? Will you ask Him to save you?

II. THE WAY OF THE FILLING

There are many who ascribe the Holy Spirit and the doctrine
of the Holy Ghost to either the Church of God or Pentecostal
denomination, and it is either misused or unused by one
denomination or another. But there is a rightful use and a rightful teaching of the doctrine of the Holy Spirit.

Our first point is the Bible way for the filling of the Holy
Spirit. There is as much confusion today about how to be filled
as there is about the command to be filled.

First, concerning the way of the filling of the Holy Spirit, there
must be desire. The Bible says in Matthew 5:6, "Blessed are they
which do hunger and thirst after righteousness: for they shall be
filled." Do you have a desire in your heart for the power of God
upon your life The sad picture of Christianity today is that there
is no desire for the power of God upon our lives. There seems to
be a self-centeredness, a self-satisfaction that has drifted across
Christianity, making us content and satisfied to be mediocre, to
be calm and cool, as it were, concerning the work of God. There is
no real desire for the anointing power of God. Unless there is a
desire to be filled with the Spirit, you will never be filled.
'Blessed is he that hungers and thirsts,' says the Scripture. This
desire must be scripturally based. That means scripturally
directed to the ear of God. If my desire is not scriptural, it will
not be answered by God. If I seek to be filled with the Spirit of
God for a sign to show that I have the Holy Spirit, then God will
not answer that prayer. God will not fill us; but it throws wide
the door, it throws wide the gate, it throws wide the opportunity
for Satan to step in and give us a false filling, to give us a false
power, a power not of God. Satan will see that we get some sort of
sign.

Remember that on the day of Pentecost the early followers
were not seeking a sign; they were waiting on power. They were
not seeking for a testimony to tell the world that they had the
Holy Spirit; they were waiting for power to tell the testimony

they already had—that Jesus is the Christ. Beware of any man or woman who brags and makes much about the fact that they have the sign that they have the Holy Ghost.

Yes, if I seek and ask God to fill me in order that I may have a sign to show that I have the Holy Ghost, then God will not answer my prayer. Satan may step in and see that we get or feel something; he may pawn off upon us that which is counterfeit and that with which we will be satisfied, but we will never experience the true filling of the Holy Spirit. "He that believeth on me, as the scripture hath said, out of his belly [innermost being] shall flow rivers of living water" (John 7:38). We must pray, our desire must be scripturally based, or God will not fill us. If I desire to be filled just to feel good, then He will not answer. I should already feel good in my soul because I am saved. No, this is not the purpose for the filling.

May I ask you today, What is your motive? what is my motive, for the filling? If it is to glorify Christ, then God will answer that prayer. If it is to do the work of God, then God will answer that prayer. He will fill me with the Spirit if it is to glorify Christ, for this is the purpose of the Holy Spirit. "For when he is come, he shall glorify me," says the Scripture.

Now the way to be filled is, first, through desire that is scripturally based. Second, our desire must be weighed carefully. Am I willing to pay the price to be filled? Am I willing to live the life of separation? Am I willing to be totally surrendered to the will of God? Am I willing to be completely submissive to the leadership of the Holy Spirit? Am I willing to be subjected to His every command? So if you pray and ask God to fill you, then your prayer must be carefully weighed.

There must not only be a desire to be filled, but there must be obedience. The Scripture says in Acts 5:29 and 32, "Then Peter and the other apostles answered and said, We ought to obey God rather than men. . . .And we are his witnesses of these things; and so is also the Holy Ghost, whom God hath given to them that obey him."

And so there must be obedience in order to be filled. A disobedient Christian will never receive the power of God.

Then there must be prayer if we are to be filled with the Holy Spirit. According to Acts 1:14, "they prayed." Then in Luke 11:13, Jesus said, ". . .how much more shall your heavenly Father give the Holy Spirit to them that ask him?" And so if you want to be filled, you must pray; and that prayer must be hearty and sincere as opposed to formal and hypocritical. Your prayer must be earnest and fervent, as opposed to cold and careless. Your prayer must be in faith and confidence, as opposed to doubting and distrust.

Today the way to be filled is by desire, by obedience, and by prayer.

III. PROOF OF THE FILLING

The command for the filling, the way of the filling is clearly seen. Now we want to study very carefully the proof of the filling. If we listen to the different groups or religious denominations, we get many different testimonies as to the proof of whether or not a man is filled with the Holy Spirit. Some groups tell us that we must speak in an unknown tongue to prove we have the Spirit. The Bible does not teach this. I will admit that according to the book of Acts, languages were spoken by the apostles, not unknown tongues; for those words—"unknown tongues"—are not in the original language. It is always in italics in the King James Bible because there is no such thing as an unknown tongue. Acts 2:8 says, "And how hear we every man in our own tongue [our own dialect], wherein we were born?" Parthians and Medes and others down through verses 11 and 12 tell how amazed they were that they heard the gospel message in their own language. This came as a result of the anointing and it was a product of the Holy Spirit. The Bible nowhere says that a man must speak in an unknown language or another language as proof that he has the Holy Spirit.

Let us remember that the early disciples were not seeking for a proof; they were only seeking for the power of God. This is what we need today. We need to ask for the power of God upon our lives, not to try to have some sort of a testimony that we have the Holy Ghost. There is nothing in the Scripture that says we must have a language. There were men gathered from all nations on that day; and God, through the Holy Spirit, gave those men the gift to speak in a language whereby those people could be saved. If we needed it today, God could do the same thing again. But the real proof of the filling of the Holy Spirit is seen in these next few things we will discuss.

A. The proof of the filling of the Spirit of God is seen in the power that was demonstrated in the lives of the early followers of Jesus Christ.

In Acts 1, they were told to wait for power. In Acts 4:33, the Bible says, "And with great power gave the apostles witness of the resurrection of the Lord Jesus: and great grace was upon them all." They needed power to preach, so they received power to preach. Peter stood up and preached as never before. Philip and Stephen stood and preached as never before. They needed power, and power came when they were filled with the Holy Ghost. They had power for witnessing, for personal testimony to the unsaved about the saving grace of God.

Homiletically, preachers today are right down the line. We have never had a day when it seems as though men were more learned, more scholarly; but we have never seen a day when men were so powerless in the pulpits. Homiletically speaking, as far as giving a beautiful, outlined sermon, men can do it; but where is the power that should be demonstrated, that should be bringing the lost down the aisles? Men are homiletically perfect but without enough power to blow the fuzz off a peach. They were told that they needed the power of God upon them.

We, as the preachers of the Gospel of Jesus Christ, who are the living witnesses of Jesus Christ, need the power of God on our lives to get the job done. If all we have to do is to play the piano at church, or to water the petunias, or to parch peanuts at brotherhood meetings and socials, then we have all the power we need. But if we are going to engage in the battle for the souls of men and meet the Devil on the battlefield, then we need more than we now have. We need that power that can only come with the Holy Spirit.

Today it seems all the average church needs is a mimeograph

machine to roll off the order of the services, to tell us when the invitation is supposed to take place, to tell us what to sing, when to pray, but with no power of God upon us. We need power of the Holy Spirit today. The power is seen only when we are filled with the Holy Spirit.

B. We have found in Acts 1 that the proof is seen in the power demonstrated in the life of the believer. Then we find, second, that the proof is seen in a holy boldness.

Acts 4:29, "And now, Lord, behold their threatenings: and grant unto thy servants, that with all boldness they may speak thy word." We read in verse 31, "And when they had prayed, the place was shaken where they were assembled together; and they were all filled with the Holy Ghost, and they spake the word of God with boldness."

When a Christian is filled with the Holy Spirit, one of the proofs of that filling is that he will speak, will witness with a holy boldness. These disciples asked that they may have the boldness with which to speak His Word. When they were filled, they were given this boldness. If there were ever a day that holy boldness is needed, it is now. This is the age of cowards. Men are afraid to stand. They have no boldness. We see them compromising on the Bible. We see them compromising on the issue of godly living. We see them compromising God's precious Word. Men today are afraid of the WMU and the other women's organizations of the church. Men are afraid today of the official church board. Today is the day of pussyfooting, compromising preachers; and there seems to be no boldness to take a real stand for God. We need today a holy boldness. And when we are filled with the Spirit of God, there will be that boldness.

C. The proof of the filling of the Holy Spirit is also seen in the oneness of believers.

Acts 2:44, "And all that believed were together, and had all things common." Now when this early church, these early believers at Pentecost, were filled with the Spirit of God, there was a oneness among them all, a oneness desperately needed today among professing Christians. The average church across this land is a divided church. There is not a oneness concerning practice, concerning praise or prayer. This early church manifested a glorious Spirit-filled oneness.

The Bible tells us in verse 42 that there was a oneness in their fellowship: "And they continued stedfastly in the apostles' doctrine and fellowship, and in breaking of bread, and in prayers." There was a oneness in their fellowship. Thank God for the people of God who can get together and have a spirit of oneness prevail in their fellowship.

There was also a oneness in their doctrine. That Scripture says, "And they continued stedfastly in the apostles' doctrine." My, how confusing today is the doctrinal issue throughout the average New Testament church.

There is not a oneness today on the doctrine of tithing. Many members are opposed to and find all manner of excuses for not putting this doctrine into practice. Consequently, there is not a oneness on the doctrine of tithing.

There is not a oneness today in the doctrine of prayer, as it is seen here in the life of these early believers (vs. 42).

Then there was a oneness about their possessions. Verse 45 says, "And sold their possessions and goods, and parted them to all men, as every man had need." Not only was there a oneness in their possessions, but there was a oneness in their purpose. Their purpose was to propogate and to present the Gospel. This they did.

D. Not only is the proof of the filling of the Holy Spirit seen in the power, and in the boldness, and in the oneness, but the proof is also seen in wisdom.

The Bible says in Acts 6, speaking of those first seven men who were chosen, "Wherefore, brethren, look ye out among you seven men of honest report, full of the Holy Ghost and wisdom" (vs. 3). There is a wisdom that goes along with the filling of the Spirit. Psalm 136:5 speaks of the wisdom of God, the same wisdom which the Lord Jesus imparts to us through the Holy Spirit. Acts 6:9,10, especially verse 10, says, "Then there arose certain of the synagogue. . .disputing with Stephen. And they were not able to resist the wisdom and the spirit by which he spake." So a godly, heavenly wisdom is manifested in the life of that person who is filled with the Holy Spirit.

Oh, how tragic to see a man who says he is filled with the Holy Spirit have no wisdom concerning the work and the Word of God. Can we accept that this man is filled with the Holy Spirit?

E. The proof of the filling of the Holy Spirit is seen in the perseverance of that believer.

The Bible says in Acts 2:42, "And they continued stedfastly . . . ." I like that. Praise the Lord for those who continue on!

The Bible teaches us that when we are filled with the Spirit, there is a continuance in our Christian life. Preachers today are quitting the ministry. Deacons are quitting the ministry. Sunday school teachers are quitting the ministry. We have never seen the like of those who are falling by the wayside. The proof that a man is full of the Holy Ghost of God is that there is a continuance in his life.

Jesus said, "If ye continue in my word, then are ye my disciples." The proof is seen in the perseverance of the saints. The perseverance of the saints continues in the light of the troubles that face them. Surely if there were ever a people who had troubles to face, those early Christians had them. If there were ever a group of Christians who continued through the trials, it was these early Christians. If there were ever Christians who continued steadfastly through persecution, then it was these early Christians. We wonder how in the world they could keep going on, in the light of the fact that they were being persecuted by the Romans, were being put to death in the Roman arenas, and were being burned at the stakes. They were being fed to wild beasts. Their bodies were being torn asunder. How could they keep on manifesting the name of Christ and be steadfast in witnessing and living for God? Only in the fullness of the Holy Spirit would they do it. You and I today can and need to continue, and the only way we can do it is with the filling of the Holy Spirit.

F. Another proof that is seen in the filling of the Holy Spirit is the Christlikeness of those who are filled.

Before the day of Pentecost, Peter's speech betrayed him. You remember the incident outside Pilate's hall. And down the road where Peter was warming his hands by the fire of the ungodly, when he was asked about his acquaintance and relationship to this man called Jesus, he cursed and swore, "I don't know Him." They said, "But your speech betrays you." Now, before Pentecost his speech betrayed him, but says Acts 4:13, "Now when they saw the boldness [which came from the filling] of Peter and John, and perceived that they were unlearned and ignorant men, they marvelled; and they took knowledge of them, that they had been with Jesus."

His life had betrayed him. When one is filled with the Spirit of God, he will carry a Christlikeness about him. Jesus will be seen in that life. To be filled with the Holy Spirit means that you and I will act like Jesus in compassion and in doing the will of God.

Yes, and we will be Christlike in soul winning. Now, if there were any one evidence that we are to seek for particular proof that a man is filled with the Spirit of God, it would be whether he is Christlike in his desire to see men saved.

Now, if we want to know how a man acts, what the results are when he is filled with the Holy Spirit, we need not speculate; we need not wonder about what happens or what is the proof. The Bible unmistakably has given proof of the filling. This was seen in the lives of those early Christians who were filled with the Holy Spirit on the day of Pentecost. How did they act? What did they do? What was the main purpose in their filling? What was the outstanding thing in their lives after Pentecost? They went after the souls of men.

Now, these men on the day of Pentecost spoke in other languages, not in an unknown tongue. They did speak with dialects, languages, and the Bible says every man heard in his own tongue the wonderful words of God. After these people were filled with the Holy Ghost, the anointing and the unusual gift of being able to speak in other languages was not the end of the filling but the means to an end.

You have missed it if you believe that the ultimate end is to be filled with the Holy Spirit. It is a means to an end. The end is that men might be saved. They were filled; they were empowered; they were given wisdom and boldness that they might ultimately **reach people without Jesus Christ.**

In Acts 2, when these men were filled, they preached for the souls of men. Peter stood up on the day of Pentecost and preached, and the Bible says in verse 8, "And how hear we every man in our own tongue, wherein we were born?" And Acts 2:7 says, "They were all amazed and marvelled" at what they heard. What did they hear? The Gospel. They heard the message of salvation and as they heard, they asked in verse 37, "Men and brethren, what shall we do?" Peter told them what to do and they did it, and they were added to the church daily, according to verse 47, such as were being saved. So the main object and the final proof of the filling of the Holy Spirit is seen in the salvation of souls.

My friend, if you say you have been filled with the Spirit of God, I do not care whether you speak in a tongue or language—or you name it—if it hasn't led you to go out into the highways and hedges, if there is not a compulsion to reach the souls of men for whom God sent His Son and for whom His Son died, then you have missed it. You have received wildfire, not the anointing and filling of the Holy Spirit of God. For when these men were filled with the Holy Spirit, they preached for the souls of men. In Acts 2:19-21 is the message that came from the filling of these early believers. The filling of the Holy Spirit is seen in the outreaching for the souls of men and women, boys and girls.

So in order to go, and in order not to let anything stand in our way, yea, even death, we must be filled with the Spirit of God.

On the day of Pentecost, as we read in Acts 1 and 2, when they were filled, they preached for the souls of men. "Repent ye therefore, and be converted, that your sins may be blotted out, when the times of refreshing shall come from the presence of the Lord; And he shall send Jesus Christ, which before was preached unto you" (Acts 3:19,20). The evidence of the filling of the Spirit is seen here in their preaching.

In Acts 4, they preached for the souls of men.

"Then Peter, filled with the Holy Ghost, said unto them, Ye rulers of the people, and elders of Israel, If we this day be ex-

amined of the good deed done to the impotent man, by what means he is made whole; Be it known unto you all, and to all the people of Israel, that by the name of Jesus Christ of Nazareth, whom ye crucified, whom God raised from the dead, even by him doth this man stand here before you whole."—Acts 4:8-10.

Verse 31 says:

"And when they had prayed, the place was shaken where they were assembled together; and they were all filled with the Holy Ghost, and they spake the word of God with boldness."

In Acts 5 they reached out for the souls of men. Verse 42, "And daily in the temple, and in every house, they ceased not to teach and preach Jesus Christ." The Bible says that every believer went everywhere reaching out for the souls of men.

In Acts 8:3,4:

"As for Saul, he made havock of the church, entering into every house, and haling men and women committed them to prison. Therefore they that were scattered abroad went every where preaching the word."

Do not be confused. The Bible makes it plain that where there is no compassion and no concern for the souls of men, there is an absence of the filling of the Holy Spirit. Where there is compassion and concern, where there is an outreach for the souls of men—this is a product of the filling of the Holy Spirit.

G. According to John 16, when He is come, Jesus said, He shall lift up and glorify the Father. In verses 13,14:

"Howbeit when he, the Spirit of truth, is come, he will guide you into all truth: for he shall not speak of himself; but whatsoever he shall hear, that shall he speak: and he will shew you things to come. He shall glorify me."

Now the mark of a Spirit-filled man is his lifting up Jesus, his bragging on Jesus, his witnessing about Jesus, his preaching Jesus. It is our ministry to join the ministry of the Holy Spirit and lift up Jesus Christ. This is the mark of the filling.

In Acts 1:21 and 22, concerning these Spirit-filled believers, we find they lifted up Jesus:

"Wherefore of these men which have companied with us all the time that the Lord Jesus went in and out among us, Beginning from the baptism of John, unto that same day that he was taken up from us, must one be ordained to be a witness with us of his resurrection."

In Acts 3:6, Peter lifted up the Lord Jesus: "Then Peter said, Silver and gold have I none; but such as I have give I thee: In the name of Jesus Christ of Nazareth rise up and walk." Now verse 26: "Unto you first God, having raised up his Son Jesus, sent him to bless you, in turning away every one of you from his iniquities."

When a man is filled with the Spirit of God, he will ultimately witness and lift up Jesus Christ. Beware of the man who brags that he has the Holy Ghost. But thank God for the man who brags on Jesus. This is the man under the influence of the Holy Spirit.

Let us who are saved seek to be filled with the blessed Holy Spirit so we may lift up our blessed Lord Jesus and see the lost saved. If you are lost, then call upon Jesus Christ to come into your heart, to forgive your sins and save you.

John 1:12 says: ". . .as many as received him, to them gave he power to become the sons of God."

CHAPTER 9

Relationship Goals

This morning I want to speak to you on "Relationship Goals."

Everyone needs a goal in life. Everyone certainly needs to be striving to attain something good in life. A business has to have goals in order to grow and succeed. I think a family has to have goals for their children and for the future. Every life needs goals which keep one striving toward a point in life.

Certainly we Christians need goals that have to do with our Christian service. To be the best teacher I can possibly be, to win more boys and girls to Christ this year, or to ask the Lord for one hundred souls this year, are worthy goals for the Christian.

We have certain goals for the church. We want to be reaching, after the first of the year, an average of one thousand in Sunday school per Sunday, believing that would honor God. God honors every goal that you set that lifts up and glorifies His Son.

There are many service goals. I have had a personal goal for a long time. I don't want to be just any old preacher, just an average preacher. My goal is to be a good preacher, a faithful pastor.

Do you have some service goals in your life?

Have you ever considered relationship goals? Have you ever set a goal in your relationship to Jesus Christ? Not in service, not something just for yourself, but a goal in your relationship to the Lord Jesus Christ.

What do you want to be just to Him? What kind of relationship would you like to enjoy with the Lord Jesus Christ?

There are two places in Scripture that I have chosen this morning which I think are outstanding. And these would be two worthy goals for us to consider. One is related to Abraham, the other to David.

After all, we are related to God. He is our heavenly Father by way of the new birth. We have no right to call God our Father unless we have been saved. Being born physically does not make God our Father. However, being born into His family makes us His children. "To as many as received him," Jesus said, "to them gave he the power to become the sons of God."

I don't know about you, but I want more of a relationship to God than just church membership or a baptismal certificate. I want that established relationship with him by way of the new birth. As Paul said, "Whereby we cry, Abba, Father."

Jesus taught His disciples to pray. When you pray—you children, you disciples, you believers—when you pray, say, "Our Father which art in heaven, Hallowed be thy name."

How blessed are you who this morning can say that you have a heavenly Father!

I. ABRAHAM—a Friend of God

There are two statements that Jesus made—one in relation to Abraham, one in relation to David—that certainly would be worthy relationship goals. The first one was made about Abraham. Abraham was called the friend of God. That's a personal relationship statement. "Abraham, my friend."

I can say that I'm acquainted with this or that person; and I can give hundreds of names, as you could; but I couldn't say of all of them, "He's my friend." When you say that, you mean he is special.

A fellow preacher said to me the other day, "I just want to tell you that you are more than just a fellow preacher; you are my personal friend." That meant something to me. Turn to Isaiah 41:8, "But thou, Israel, art my servant, Jacob whom I have chosen, the seed of Abraham my friend."

He didn't just say, "Abraham, through whom I chose to build a nation," or, "Abraham, that great man of faith." Rather, he said, "Abraham, my friend." That statement drew my attention to Abraham in a special way. That made me wonder what Abraham did that God the Almighty, the Creator of the u- niverse, the Holder of mankind's destiny, would say of this human being, "He is My friend." To be the friend of God is a worthy goal right there.

Now turn to James 2:21-23:

"Was not Abraham our father justified by works, when he had offered Isaac his son upon the altar? Seest thou how faith wrought with his works, and by works was faith made perfect? And the scripture was fulfilled which saith, Abraham believed God, and it was imputed unto him for righteousness: and he was called the Friend of God."

If we are righteous today in God's sight, it is because He has imputed to us His righteousness. We have no righteousness of our own. We are not born with righteousness. We can't buy righteousness. There is nothing we can do to make ourselves righteous. The Bible says, "All our righteousness is as filthy rags" in the sight of God. If we, like Abraham, have any righteousness, it is because it has been imputed to us, given to us on the basis that Jesus Christ, God's Son, died upon the cross for us. When we receive Him as our personal Saviour, we are counted righteous in God's sight.

But while we may be righteous in God's sight—and all of us who are saved are—yet He said of Abraham, "He is My friend." He didn't say that about all to whom He had imputed righteousness.

Now, let's look at two things: the wonder and the prospect of Abraham's being a friend of God. There is a prospect for you and me to become the friend of God even as did Abraham. But the wonder of it is just simply a declaration of fact, a declaration of the fact Abraham was called the friend of God. What a testimony for you and me if others could look at us and say, "That man is the friend of God. God is his friend"! Abraham, no doubt, was called a friend because there was a mutual trust between God and him.

I said to my wife about Dusty, Brother Grubbs, and Brother Cox, "These men are more than just associates in the work; they are good friends." To have a friend laboring with you makes for a good relationship. Dusty is my friend because I trust him and he trusts me. We uphold one another. I don't do a whole lot with the youth work; I just trust Brother Dusty, knowing that what he does will be good. He is a friend.

You may not trust a fellow who is not your friend; but when you declare one to be a good friend, you will trust him. God trusted in Abraham, as we see from Genesis 18:17-19:

"And the Lord said, Shall I hide from Abraham that thing which I do; Seeing that Abraham shall surely become a great and mighty nation, and all the nations of the earth shall be blessed in him? For I know him, that he will command his children and his household after him, and they shall keep the way of the Lord, to do justice and judgment; that the Lord may bring upon Abraham that which he hath spoken of him."

He said of Abraham, "I know that he will bring up his children right. I know that he will teach his family right. I can depend on Abraham to say and do the right thing in his household."

Could you be a friend of God? Could God trust you? Could God say of you, "I know that he will command his children"? That doesn't mean that always children will do what we command, but we have a responsibility under God to command them in the ways of God.

Some say, "Well, I don't think you ought to make children do anything." Stop making them brush their teeth? Stop commanding them to go to bed at a certain time? Stop commanding them to go certain places and not go other places? Or eating the things they ought to eat?

No! No! No! It's right to instruct your children in the things of God. Husband, it's right to command your family. It is right for a man to command his wife in the things of God. She is to be obedient unto the husband in those things. Lady, if your husband wants to serve God and you don't, then you are being disobedient unto God. You are being rebellious unto God.

"I know Abraham; he is My friend. I can trust Abraham. I know that he will command his children." It was important that Abraham start that way because he was going to be the head of a nation. But God could trust Abraham, and Abraham trusted God. They had a mutual trust. (Many things could be said about the trust of Abraham, but I don't have time to explore them this morning.) Certainly Abraham trusted God, and God trusted Abraham.

The book of Romans states that Abraham staggered not at the promises of God. Nothing shook Abraham. He just kept right on walking, right on believing, right on trusting. He trusted God when God gave him some hard things to do. He knew he could trust God. When God said, "Abraham, I want you to take your only son, Isaac, up to the mountain. There you are to offer him as a sacrifice unto Me," Abraham didn't question that any more than he did the day God said, "Abraham, leave your home and family and come with Me out of the Ur of the Chaldees. I will make of you a great nation." Abraham took off—not knowing where he was going, but he was being obedient unto God. "He staggered not at the promises of God."

When God told Abraham to take his son up on the mountain, he got his son and the wood and set out. He kept moving without hesitation or question. He trusted explicitly and completely in God. Although he did not understand it, yet he had no questions or reservations about it. Though he found it heart-rending to offer his own son, yet he questioned not but went forward without hesitation until God stayed his hand. Just as the knife was drawn back to be plunged into his boy's heart, God said, "Wait!"

Why, it is no wonder God said of Abraham, "He is My friend." No wonder they should have such a friendship.

Not only was there trust, but there was constant communion. It is hard to maintain a good friendship if there is not constant communion. Dusty is my friend every week. Brother Cox is my friend every week. Brother Grubbs is my friend every week. My wife is my wife every week. You understand she's more than a friend. Friendship means a constant communion.

The Bible says that the Lord visited Abraham. Don't you like to go see a friend?

Then in Genesis 19:27, notice that Abraham had communion with God: "And Abraham gat up early in the morning to the place where he stood before the Lord."

No wonder God said of Abraham, "He is My friend." Brother, when you get up early every morning and go stand before God and talk with Him, you are seeking to be God's friend. Every man needs a place where he can go and stand before God every day. Because of this constant communion, Abraham and God were friends.

Turn to Genesis 14:21-23. I don't have time to relate all of the story here, but Abraham had helped a needy king. He brought his own personal army and his servants and helped the king of Sodom. Now the king wanted to repay Abraham with lavish gifts for his help, but Abraham refused for one reason:

"And the king of Sodom said unto Abram, Give me the persons, and take the goods to thyself."

He is saying, "Let me have the captives, but all of the spoils of the victory, keep them for yourself."

"And Abram said to the king of Sodom, I have lift up mine hand unto the Lord, the most high God, the possessor of heaven and earth, That I will not take from a thread even to a shoelatchet, and that I will not take any thing that is thine, lest thou shouldest say, I have made Abram rich."

He wanted the king to know that God was the one who blessed him. He was jealous for the glory of God. "What I have, God has given to me. God has blessed me with it." When a man who wants to commune with God will go and stand before God and be jealous with the way he lives and with the substance that comes his way, so that God gets all of the glory, he will not stagger at the promises of God. It is no wonder that God would say of him, "He is My friend."

You could be a friend of God. I could be a friend of God. I want you to look at John 15:14,15. There Jesus made these statements:

"Ye are my friends, if ye do whatsoever I command you. Henceforth I call you not servants; for the servant knoweth not

*what his lord doeth: but I have called you friends; for all things
that I have heard of my Father I have made known unto you."*

Would you set a relationship goal to be a friend of God? Would
you look at verse 14 and consider all that it implies? Would you
say that by the grace of God you want to do whatever has to be
done to be a friend of God?

I want to be more than just a servant, more than just a
preacher, more than just a church member. I would like for God
to be able to say of me, "He is My friend. My friend." What did
He say? "This is my commandment, That ye love one another,
as I have loved you" (vs. 12). Would you be willing to love as you
ought to love in order to be the friend of God? Jesus said in verse
14, "Ye are my friends, if ye do whatsoever I command you." He
is saying, "Would you do that just to be My friend?" Would you,
like Abraham, not stagger at any command?

The Bible says there is a crown for faithfulness. If He commands you to be faithful and not forsake the house of God, would
you obey in order to be a friend of God? "As my Father has sent
me, even so send I you." Would you comply with that command
just to be His friend? Would you be the friend of God? Would you
be jealous just for His glory in order to be His friend?

To be God's friend is a great prospect, but obedience is the
main key to that friendship. The Bible says that to obey is better
than sacrifice. One of the greatest things a friend could do for me
would be to do what I ask. Though it may cost something, yet if
he is my friend and loves me, he will do it.

Sometimes the price of friendship may seem too hard for him.
Some say, "Lord, if these are the conditions of friendship, I don't
think I want to be Your friend. If being Your friend demands my
being faithful, my living clean, moral and upright—no, I can't do
that."

"Come out from among them, and be ye separate, saith the
Lord." Would we comply with that command in order to be a
friend of God? Or do we say, "No, Lord. If that is the basis for
friendship, then I certainly couldn't do it"?

If you are saved, you have a relationship. Do you have a goal in that relationship? Is there a goal you have set for your own personal life, a goal just between you and the Lord Jesus?

Abraham was called a friend of God. This is the first relationship goal. A second goal is to be a man after God's own heart.

II. DAVID—a Man After God's Own Heart

Notice in I Samuel 13:14: "But now thy kingdom shall not continue: the Lord hath sought him a man after his own heart."

God was speaking to King Saul. Saul had disobeyed Him. He found that God was more pleased with obedience than sacrifice. It is much more important for us to obey the Lord than to give a lot of money or do other things. To sacrifice or give up things just for God is not enough. Obedience is what the Lord wants. We found that the obedience that was so important in Abraham's life is just as important in ours. The whole key is *obedience.* "Ye are my friends, if ye do whatsoever I command you."

In addition, God said to Saul, 'Saul, a man is going to come and take the place that you now hold. Your kingdom is coming to an end. I have found another man, a man after My own heart.'

Why would God say that about David? The prophet had gone to the home of Jesse to find a new man to anoint king. Through the story we learn that Saul was not indispensable. That is true of Christians, too. God always has another man on the scene ready to go if we fail.

The prophet went to the home of Jesse. All of the sons were brought out for the prophet to review. Finally, the one who was least likely to be king—a little red-headed, ruddy-faced lad— came in by the name of David. They didn't even consider him; but the prophet said, "He is the one," and anointed him with the oil. Look at Acts 13:22:

"And when he had removed him, he raised up unto them David to be their king; to whom also he gave testimony, and said, I have found David the son of Jesse, a man after mine own heart, which shall fulfil all my will."

Though David sinned, he was to fulfill the will of God. And so it is recorded for us both in the Old Testament and in the New that David was a man after God's own heart. Probably no other Bible character more fully demonstrates for us the moral range of the human heart and human nature.

How close to God, how dedicated, how sold out we can be for God; how ready we can be to stand up even at the cost of our lives, yet, in another instant fall into sin and be counted out of the race. Human nature encompasses many possibilities of sin and failure. Were it not for the grace of God, neither you nor I would be in the race tonight. We might be out in the world.

Look at Psalm 23. *"The Lord is my shepherd;* [He said a lot when he said that.] *I shall not want.* [That showed his utter dependence upon God, his willingness to look to God to bring him in and out to find pastures.] *He maketh me to lie down in green pastures:* [That spoke of his obedience to God.] *he leadeth me beside the still waters.* [He brings me to the peaceable places in my life.] *He restoreth my soul:* [When I'm down, God lifts me up.] *he leadeth me in the paths of righteousness for his name's sake. Yea, though I walk through the valley of the shadow of death, I will fear no evil: for thou art with me; thy rod and thy staff they comfort me.* [An awareness of the presence of God in his life.] *Thou preparest a table before me in the presence of mine enemies: thou anointest my head with oil; my cup runneth over.* [The gladness of God in his soul.] *Surely goodness and mercy shall follow me all the days of my life: and I will dwell in the house of the Lord for ever."*

Confidence in God. It is hard to believe that the man who wrote that Psalm and many others is the man who fell into sin with Bath-sheba. This man got so deep into sin until he finally had to make out a plan whereby Bath-sheba's husband could be killed.

Somehow, I think, we have emphasized the *sin* of David and have forgotten the good he accomplished. Sometimes we want to pick out the bad and forget about all the good that he did for God. We all have a tendency to do that. Our nature causes us to forget all the good a man does and write him off for one mistake, one error, one wrong deed. One bad encounter makes us forget all the good he has ever done.

That can happen to preachers, too. A pastor can labor, work, pray and cry with families; then let one little thing go wrong and he is written off, set off to the side. Unfortunately, our nature causes us to forget all the good somebody does.

I was talking to our bus director about this recently. We had worked with a family for a long time. The bus director had brought the children to church for a long time and had finally gotten the whole family coming. But when the children missed a Sunday and the Sunday school teachers called to check on the child and to let the parents know that they were missed, the parents took it that the teacher was prying into their business. The family told me when I visited them that they were not coming back because we pried into their business.

This family forgot about all of the hours and Sundays that the bus director had gotten up early, prayed over those kids, and l ad gone out and brought them in to Sunday school. They had forgotten about the children hearing the Gospel taught and preached here. They just marked us off. Why? That is human nature.

It is human nature to forget all the goodness and fall out with one over the bad in his life. We may have done that with David. Oh, listen! God does not condone sin, and neither do we. No righteous man, no, not even an angel in Heaven, would condone David's sin; but let us not forget the good that David did. Even after David's sin is recorded, let us not forget that God refers to David as a man after His own heart.

Let's think for a moment about the goodness in David's life, his character, and the reasons that to be a man after God's own heart is a worthy goal.

Certainly, as God speaks favorably of David, He is speaking of the accomplishment for good and all that was right in David's life. Turn to I Kings 14:8: "And rent the kingdom away from the house of David, and gave it thee: and yet thou has not been as my servant David, who kept my commandments, and who followed me with all his heart, to do that only which was right in mine eyes."

The prophet is referring to the kingdom change here, but notice that he is also saying that David did far more right than wrong. You and I can learn a lesson from this. As Christians, remember that any of us at any moment may do wrong. But let us love one another for who we are and for what we have done that was right and good. Help that one if he does wrong. Instead of marking him off, love him and try to help restore him to the place that he might have been for God.

In this passage, God reminded the new king Jeroboam that he had not been as King David who kept His commandments with all his heart and did that which was right in the sight of God. David wrote many of the Psalms. No greater poetry has ever been written. No other poetry has been used as the Psalms have. James 5:13 states: *"Is any among you afflicted? let him pray. Is any merry? let him sing psalms."*

At times we sing from Psalm 23:

> **Surely goodness and mercy shall follow me**
> **All the days, all the days of my life;**
> **Surely goodness and mercy shall follow me**
> **All the days of my life.**
> **And I shall dwell in the house of the Lord forever,**
> **And I shall feast at the table spread for me;**
> **Surely goodness and mercy shall follow me**
> **All the days, all the days of my life.**

Brother Lester Roloff sings a lot of the Psalms. It seems the Psalms have a way of lifting and soothing the heart. God the Holy Spirit touched David's heart, and he was used to pen many beautiful passages.

David, a young man of character, was ready to give his life for his God. When others wouldn't meet Goliath on the battlefield and put their lives on the line for God or their country, David did. David asked, "Who is this guy? What is his name?" Someone answered, "He is Goliath, the giant."

Because this great giant defied and defamed the name of God, David was ready to fight and die, if need be, to stand up for his God.

You and I can be Christians after God's own heart if we are willing to sacrifice our lives, or whatever, for the honor of the name of God. Unfortunately, many Christians do not honor His name. It is shocking to hear professing Christians use the name of God in vain. A man who has been saved should change his language. O believer, if you curse or swear, ask God to forgive you and correct the problem.

When David heard Goliath, he probably thought the Israelite soldiers were standing in line to defend the name of the God of Israel. Now, in the truest sense of the word, God doesn't need anybody to defend Him; He can take care of Himself. But we should be ready and willing to stand up for Him. He stood up for us on Calvary. Paul said, "Fight the good fight." We are to reverence and honor the name of God. In this day we should be ready to lay our lives on the line for the honor of God and the testimony of Jesus Christ.

Too often Christians will go along with anything. They will work at a place which is dishonest and keep their mouths shut because they don't want to put anything on the line. David wasn't that way. He said, "I'll fight the giant."

"What do you have to fight with, David?"

"A sling shot. But I think I can handle him."

"No, you need Saul's equipment."

And when they tried to put Saul's great big armor on that little boy David, he told them, "I can't use this. I have never proven this armor." I think we ought to work with what works for us. David said of his sling shot, "I know it works. Let me use this."

You have to love David. You have to thank God for that little lad. Yes, David sinned later. But he is the same fellow who was willing to stand alone on the battlefield and go against the enemy who cursed God. Nobody else was doing it. With the help of God, David did what the others were not willing to do.

Today, backslidden Christians need to come out of the shadows and go into the arena to fight some of the giants who dare to defy God. Too many want to sit in the bleachers. They would like the worst sinners in town to be saved, but they do not want to talk with them. They don't want more bars in town, but they don't want to take a stand against alcohol. They would like for things to be better in their nation and community, but they will not raise their voice or take their stand for God against Satan.

Not only was David courageous, but he was kind and thoughtful. This quality also made David worthy to be called a man after God's own heart.

David was a kind king who did not think only of self. After he was anointed king of Israel, King Saul was jealous because he knew that his kingdom would be destroyed.

Saul had a son named Jonathan. David and Jonathan were close friends and loved each other with a true love. However, Jonathan and his father, Saul, were killed in battle; so David became king. As the new king, he had power to kill anyone related to King Saul; but instead David showed kindness to the remaining family members.

Look at II Samuel 9:1: "And David said, Is there yet any that is left of the house of Saul. . . ?"

Notice David's thoughtfulness toward the household of Saul. King Saul had been David's bitterest enemy and had tried to kill David. Yet, David was asking, 'Is there yet left any of the house of Saul that I may show kindness for Jonathan's sake?' David remembered his promise to Jonathan.

When it was learned that Jonathan had a surviving son by the name of Mephibosheth, David sent for Mephibosheth, who considered himself a dog in the sight of David because he was of the family of Saul. Look at II Samuel 9:7-9,13.

"And David said unto him, Fear not: for I will surely shew thee kindness for Jonathan thy father's sake, and will restore thee all the land of Saul thy father; and thou shalt eat bread at my table continually. And he bowed himself, and said, What is thy servant, that thou shouldest look upon such a dead dog as I am? Then the king called to Ziba, Saul's servant, and said unto him, I have given unto thy master's son all that pertained to Saul and to all his house. . . . So Mephibosheth dwelt in Jerusalem: for he did eat continually at the king's table; and was lame on both his feet."

David found this crippled young man, brought him out of obscurity, set him at the king's table, and fed him continually.

That is what our God has done for us. We were not friends of

God, but enemies, alienated from Him. However, we made peace with God through Jesus Christ. One of these days Jesus is coming for us. He will take us to His Home and set us at the marriage supper of the Lamb. Thus, we will sit at the King's table and feast with Him continually.

It doesn't hurt to be kind just as David was kind. Our churches would be better off if we showed more kindness one to another. So much of the time we are so greedy that we do not have time to be kind, or else we think it will cost too much. You will be a happier Christian if you show kindness to others.

Though David was generally a very spiritual and dedicated man, yet sin did overpower him. David's downfall began, first, by being in the wrong place at the wrong time. When the men went to war, David stayed at home. Do you remember the saying, "An idle mind is the devil's workshop"? When a person is busy, he is less likely to get into trouble, less likely to be critical, and less likely to go into sin.

One night, when David could not sleep, he went out on the roof top. From there he could see a woman bathing. The trap was set. Keep in mind that David was not looking for a woman; neither was Bath-sheba trying to ensnare a man; but the temptation was there for David. He should have turned and gone the other way. Sin is powerful and can wreck and ruin the mighty as well as the weak.

You ladies do not know how powerful the look is to a man. It is different with a woman. I'll just say this. A man can be tempted much quicker with the eye than a woman can. Many times a man's downfall is with the look, but with a woman it's the touch. That is why you ladies ought to be fair and just to the males. God made men handsome, but He made women beautiful. For women to expose their beauty in the wrong way is a sin against God. Ladies, I am not saying that it is wrong for you to have your hair fixed, nor wrong for you to wear makeup or nice clothes. But when you start putting the emphasis on your body, with your tight clothes, less clothes, and showing more of the leg, then it is a sin. Run that slit in the side of your dress up a little higher and you will have to meet God with that sin. Men will have to meet God for looking the second time, or the third, and falling.

There is a reason why the Bible says women ought to adorn themselves in modest apparel. As far as I am concerned, the most modest apparel that a woman can wear is a dress—and enough dress. Ladies should not try to fit 150 pounds in a 100 pound bag. Nor should you try to put six feet into a three-foot bag.

Again I say, man will go down with his look and woman with the touch. Because of this, young people, watch out. Petting will lead to your ruin. You girls, watch out. There is a reason why boys want to pet. They know that it stirs you and arouses your feelings. Petting does that. But man is stirred by the look.

David got into trouble when he looked. He fell into the sin of adultery. One would think that after committing adultery, David would not be called a man after God's own heart. But the New Testament describes David—a man after God's own heart. I think the reason David could still be called that is found in Psalm 51 where he repented and returned to the Lord. This shows character on David's part.

Because a person falls into sin does not mean that he has to stay there. Notice what David said in Psalm 51:5,6:

"Behold, I was shapen in iniquity; and in sin did my mother conceive me. Behold, thou desirest truth in the inward parts: and in the hidden part thou shalt make me to know wisdom."

David confessed his sin which may have been hidden to other people but not to God. Notice David's prayer about his sin and failure. This prayer shows his humility and his coming back to God:

"Purge me with hyssop, and I shall be clean: wash me, and I shall be whiter than snow. Make me to hear joy and gladness; that the bones which thou hast broken may rejoice. Hide thy face from my sins, and blot out all mine iniquities. Create in me a clean heart, O God; and renew a right spirit within me."—Vss. 7-10.

It takes something, when a person has sinned and done wrong, to come back to the Lord, to confess to God, "Lord, I'm dirty. Cleanse me. Wash me. I want to be whiter than snow. Lord,

Thou hast broken me. Forgive me and create in me a clean heart." David's heart had been tainted with his sin. He could not get away from it, but he could confess it. After confession, David made this request and promise:

"Restore unto me the joy of thy salvation; and uphold me with thy free spirit. Then will I teach transgressors thy ways; and sinners shall be converted unto thee."—Vss. 12,13.

David still wanted to be used of God. I think this is the reason that God described David as a man after His own heart. David wanted to follow God's will. David had been willing to sacrifice his life to defend the name of his God. He was a good king, a great champion and leader of Israel. Sin got into David's life, but he came back to the Lord.

Because of his sin, David suffered great loss. He sowed to the wind and reaped a whirlwind. He saw his daughter raped. He saw one son murder the rapist. Then he saw his son turn against him and try to steal the kingdom. He also saw his son Absalom die in his rebellion. David cried, "O my son Absalom, my son, my son Absalom! would God I had died for thee, O Absalom, my son, my son!" David suffered many heartaches. But he came back to God to make things right between him and God.

Many Christians have lost the joy of their salvation because of sin. They come to church and sit solemnly from week to week, unmoved. But they are not happy. They have not lost their salvation but they have lost the joy of their salvation. Brother, David was not willing for his sin nor its consequences to keep him down. He wanted his sin forgiven and the joy of the Lord restored in his heart.

What do you want in your relation with God? You ought to want to be right with Him. You ought to want to be a good Christian and soul winner. But, what do you want to be to God? Would you want to be a friend of God as Abraham was? Would you want to be a man after God's own heart as David was?

Some of you are already out of the race and you think you are out for good. But the only thing now keeping you from serving the Lord is your unwillingness to pray the prayer, "Lord, I'm a sinner. I have sinned. Cleanse me. Make me to hear joy and gladness"—a prayer David prayed after sin had taken away his joy.

Are you saved, but sour? Has sin taken away all your happiness? I determined a long time ago that I wasn't going to let anybody or any group keep me from being happy in my Christian service. If the people with whom I worked would not let me be happy, then I would just go where I could be happy. I wouldn't let anybody put something in my craw that I could not get out and be happy in the Lord. My wife of thirty-four years can tell you that. I am not going to let anybody steal what I have in the Lord. And, oh, I pray that I'll not let sin take it away.

We are all susceptible to sin. There is none who is immune to sin. There is not a man who can say that he is immune to David's sin. Man is affected by the temptations of the flesh. Now, some of the self-righteous fellows may tell you that it doesn't bother them to look, as David did. A deacon told me one time that it did not bother him for ladies to wear bikinis and march down the street in that attire. But I say that it is wrong. You and I are just as susceptible as any other man—just as susceptible as David was. Any one of you ladies or girls is just as subject to fall into sin as Bath-sheba was. But if you do fall, thank God

There is a fountain filled with blood
Drawn from Immanuel's veins;
And sinners, plunged beneath that flood,
Lose all their guilty stains.

Will you set a personal goal to be God's friend, a child after God's own heart? May our blessed Saviour help us to pay whatever price is necessary to reach these relationship goals.

CHAPTER 10

Regretful Retreats

The children of Israel were led out of Egypt to go to a promised land, a land of milk and honey. There would be difficulties along the way, but God would take care of the difficulties. He gave them protection and provision for their journey. In addition, the law which would govern their life and also their worship was given at Sinai. The Tabernacle plans were also given.

God prepared them for this land of promise and He gave them visible leadership along the way. When the Tabernacle was reared up, the cloud rested over the Tabernacle. When the cloud lifted, they were to move. When the cloud rested, they were to rest. Let's read Number 9:15-23:

"And on the day that the tabernacle was reared up the cloud covered the tabernacle, namely, the tent of the testimony: and at even there was upon the tabernacle as it were the appearance of fire, until the morning. So it was alway: the cloud covered it by day, and the appearance of fire by night. And when the cloud was taken up from the tabernacle, then after that the children of Israel journeyed: and in the place where the cloud abode, there the children of Israel pitched their tents. At the commandment of the Lord the children of Israel journeyed, and at the commandment of the Lord they pitched: as long as the cloud abode upon the tabernacle they rested in their tents. And when the cloud tarried long upon the tabernacle many days, then the children of Israel kept the charge of the Lord, and journeyed not. And so it was, when the cloud was a few days upon the taber-

nacle; according to the commandment of the Lord they abode in their tents, and according to the commandment of the Lord they journeyed. And so it was, when the cloud abode from even unto the morning, and that the cloud was taken up in the morning, then they journeyed: whether it was by day or by night that the cloud was taken up, they journeyed. Or whether it were two days, or a month, or a year, that the cloud tarried upon the tabernacle, remaining thereon, the children of Israel abode in their tents, and journeyed not: but when it was taken up, they journeyed. At the commandment of the Lord they rested in the tents, and at the commandment of the Lord they journeyed: they kept the charge of the Lord, at the commandment of the Lord by the hand of Moses."

At Kadesh-Barnea, spies were sent out into the land of milk and honey; but upon their return, a sad event develops. What could have been the final step to victory and to the promised land ended in a regretful retreat. Look at their retreat in Numbers 14:1-4:

"And all the congregation lifted up their voice, and cried; and the people wept that night. And all the children of Israel murmured against Moses and against Aaron: and the whole congregation said unto them, Would God that we had died in the land of Egypt! or would God we had died in this wilderness! And wherefore hath the Lord brought us unto this land, to fall by the sword, that our wives and our children should be prey? were it not better for us to return into Egypt? And they said one to another, Let us make a captain, and let us return into Egypt."

Let us examine this account and the reason for their retreat. Likewise, let us make some application to our own lives.

I. THE REQUEST

There are four things which I think are important about the event at Kadesh-Barnea. First, a request was made. God directed Moses to send a man from each tribe to spy out the land. Notice the text, beginning in Numbers chapter 13 verses 1,2:

"And the Lord spake unto Moses, saying, Send thou men, that

they may search the land of Canaan, which I give unto the children of Israel."

This is a very important phrase—". . .which I give." If God gives a thing, all we have to do is receive it. "For God so loved the world, that he gave his only begotten Son. . . ." I do not have to fight for salvation. The fight has already been won. Jesus has already licked the Devil. He came victorious out of the grave. Salvation is mine for the receiving.

This was their land. God said He would give it; now all they had to do was receive it and go in and possess it. Verses 17-20 of Numbers chapter 13:

"And Moses sent them to spy out the land of Canaan, and said unto them, Get you up this way southward, and go up into the mountain: And see the land, what it is, and the people that dwelleth therein, whether they be strong or weak, few or many; And what the land is that they dwell in, whether it be good or bad; and what cities they be that they dwell in, whether in tents, or in strong holds; And what the land is, whether it be fat or lean, whether there be wood therein, or not. And be ye of good courage, and bring of the fruit of the land. Now the time was the time of the firstripe grapes."

Keep in mind that the Lord told Moses, "I want you to send them out into the land." Moses came to the people and gave them God's request to go into the land. However, the spies were not sent in to determine whether or not Israel could conquer the land; they simply had to go in to possess it. God had already given it to them.

I believe God simply wanted to send out those messengers to let them see all that was there. Yes! They would see giants there. God knew that. Yes! They would see difficulties there. Yes! God knew that, too.

God is not trying to withhold from us that there are giants and difficulties out there, but He says the land can be yours. I believe God sent the spies into the land to see that everything was as He said it would be.

The spies saw that the land was as God promised. Numbers 13:23 states:

"And they came into the brook of Eshcol, and cut down from thence a branch with one cluster of grapes, and they bare it between two upon a staff. . . ."

Now, brother, those are healthy grapes! When I first read that, I thought perhaps they brought one whole length of that vineyard with them. I mean, they must have taken the whole thing! The Bible says they put a pole on one shoulder; they put a pole on the other shoulder, and they brought the cluster of grapes back between them. They brought pomegranates and figs, also. And they came out of the land.

II. THE REPORT

The second thing I want you to see is the report which was given. This is very, very important in your life and mine.

1. IT BROUGHT TRUTH: First, all of the spies brought forth a truthful report. Look at it in Numbers 13:25-27:

"And they returned from searching of the land after forty days. And they went and came to Moses, and to Aaron, and to all the congregation of the children of Israel, unto the wilderness of Paran, to Kadesh; and brought back word unto them, and unto all the congregation, and shewed them the fruit of the land. And they told him, and said, We came unto the land whither thou sentest us, and surely it floweth with milk and honey; and this is the fruit of it."

So, they came back with a truthful report. They said it is exactly as God said it would be. Sure it was; God cannot lie. God is not a man that He breaks His promises or that He lies. God cannot lie. If God tells you there is fruit abundant in the Christian life, the fruit is there; and you can have it. It is yours.

So the spies brought back a truthful report. They brought back the grapes and pomegranates—everything. As the people looked at the fruit in amazement, maybe they were about to say, "Man, I'm telling you, we have finally arrived! This is the day we have been waiting for! It's been a year since we left Egypt. Now we are finally here. Have you ever seen such pomegranates! Look at those figs! Look at those grapes! Man, let us go!"

2. IT BROUGHT DOUBT: Unfortunately, the spies also brought back doubt and discouragement. About the time the whole two million Israelites were surveying the beauty of the fruit from the land of milk and honey, somebody said, "NEVERTHELESS. . . ." In my Bible, I have drawn a ring around the first word of Numbers 13:28—"NEVERTHELESS." Boy! Those "neverthelesses" will kill you! Brother, those "neverthelesses" can stymie and stagnate a lot of churches! "Well, now you can see this IS out there, but. . . !" That's why you can believe some of the sheep are not sheep, but goats. BUT!

"Nevertheless the people be strong that dwell in the land, [However, those people are not stronger than God.] *and the cities are walled* [But not a wall that God can't bring down.] *and very great:* [But not as great as God.] *and moreover, we saw the children of Anak there.* [The children of Anak certainly are not stronger than the children of God.] *The Amalekites dwell in the land of the south: and the Hittites, and the Jebusites, and the Amorites, dwell in the mountains: and the Canaanites dwell by the sea, and by the coast of Jordan."*

And they saw the Jebusites and the Amalekites and the Hittites and the Jebusites and every other kind of "ite" by the river, by the sea, by the mountain, by the clusters of grapes, by the pomegranates, and by the figs. Here was a giant; there was an Amalekite or a Jebusite. Everywhere somebody was standing in the way of getting the blessings that God had prepared for them.

You mark it down! In your Christian life, the Devil will always have something in the way to keep you from getting any blessing that God has in store.

The spies brought a discouraging report—"NEVERTHELESS." But there are two men I want you to look at—Joshua and Caleb. After hearing the discouraging report of the other spies, Caleb stilled the people. I can hear the people murmuring; and while they were muttering, Caleb said, "Now, wait a minute. Keep your mouth shut. Listen here!" And Caleb stilled the people before Moses and said, "Let us go up at once." Thank God for somebody who has faith enough to believe that God can effect the victory. "Let us go up at once, and possess it; for we are well able to overcome it." Anything that is in the land—whether it be a Jebusite, or an Amorite, or whatever—if God be for us, who can be against us? Caleb said, "Let's go."

Brother, this is not the time to murmur. This is not the time to complain. This is not the time to doubt. This is the time to get up and go!

There are far too few who are ready to possess the things that God would give and has given us. Far too few are ready to claim God's promises. Far too many in our congregations doubt that God can do a great work for His glory in this age and for this generation. **Great things can be done for Him.**

Caleb and Joshua said, "Let's go; it can be done," but the people became irate. Most people are prone to be doubters and follow the "NEVERTHELESS" crowd. Few are in the Caleb crowd, ready to possess God's promises.

Thinking that Joshua and Caleb would lead them into disaster, the irate crowd was ready to stone both men.

Notice what happened in Numbers 14:6-8:

"And Joshua the son of Nun, and Caleb the son of Jephunneh, which were of them that searched the land, rent their clothes: And they spake unto all the company of the children of Israel, saying, The land, which we passed through to search it, is an exceeding good land. If the Lord delight in us, then he will bring us into this land. . . ."

That is the key right there. "If the Lord delight in us, then he will bring us into this land. . . ." Who will bring us there? God will. You know who opened up the Jordan River? God did. Brother, it wasn't the Raft Committee that figured out a way to get across. God opened up Jordan. Ladies and gentlemen, who made the Red Sea open? It was God. Who brought the walls of Jericho down? It was God. He fights our battles and gives the victory.

And Joshua and Caleb said:

"If the Lord delight in us, then he will bring us into this land, and give it us; a land which floweth with milk and honey. Only rebel not ye against the Lord, neither fear ye the people of the land; for they are bread for us: their defence is departed from them, and the Lord is with us: fear them not.—Vss. 8,9.

We need some men in this generation who recognize that this business is God's business and the Lord is with us. Read verse 10:

"But all the congregation bade stone them with stones. And the glory of the Lord appeared in the tabernacle of the congregation before all the children of Israel."

The report brought the truth. The spies brought the grapes— and they brought their doubts. The report also brought something else. . .

3. THE ANGER OF GOD: The disbelief of the children of Israel brought the anger of God. God said, "Why, that doubtful people! Why, those discouraging people! Why, that 'nevertheless crowd,' that faithless crowd!" God said, "I'll just wipe the whole bunch out. I'll just kill them all." Read with me Numbers 14:11,12:

"And the Lord said unto Moses, How long will this people provoke me? and how long will it be ere they believe me, for all the signs which I have shewed among them? I will smite them with the pestilence, and disinherit them, and will make of thee a greater nation and mightier than they."

The people brought on the anger of God. I wonder if God isn't sorely displeased with us so much of the time because we do not believe Him? Let me ask you a question: Do you honestly believe, in this day when Atlanta, Georgia, is one of the worst cities in the world as far as morality is concerned, that God can build a great work in this place? Do you really believe that? Brother, I believe it. If we can be a people that God can delight in, if we pray and live so that we are God's delight, He will give us the "land." He will give us a great victory.

4. IT BROUGHT INTERCESSION BY MOSES: This report brought intercession as Moses pled with God for an unbelieving

people. God said, "I am going to kill them all. I am going to wipe them all out." Thank God for Moses who prayed! I wonder if in this day God would not kill part of our congregations if it were not for some who pray. Who was the intercessor? Verses 13 and 14 state it was Moses:

"And Moses said unto the Lord, Then the Egyptians shall hear it, (for thou broughtest up this people in thy might from among them;) And they will tell it to the inhabitants of this land: for they have heard that thou Lord art among this people, that thou Lord art seen face to face, and that thy cloud standeth over them, and that thou goest before them, by daytime in a pillar of cloud, and in a pillar of fire by night."

Moses was pleading for his people. Because of the interceding of Moses, God spared that people that day. Those people stood on the very brink of the judgment of God. However, a man of God went to prayer. He said, "Lord, I pray for this people. Do not destroy them." Look at verses 19 and 20: "Pardon, I beseech thee, the iniquity of this people according unto the greatness of thy mercy, and as thou hast forgiven this people, from Egypt until now. And the Lord said, I have pardoned according to thy word."

Thy word, Moses.

Do you know why we are here today? Did you know that every night this week at 6:00 some people will be in our prayer room praying? Did you know that forty men were here this morning praying as they do every Sunday morning? People were in prayer meetings this past Tuesday night praying. Doing what? Interceding! "O, God, spare that one, revive that one! Save the unsaved!" That's what we are here for. Where is that one who will do the interceding?

III. THE RETREAT

A third word to notice in this passage is retreat. Involved in this event were a request, a report, and a retreat. To whom did the people listen? To Joshua? No. To Caleb? No. Instead of listening to these two men, they listened to the other ten. The people decided that instead of advancing, they would retreat. They saw the fruit of the land. They had also seen the power of God, but they would not go in.

God said, "Will these people. . .how long ere they believe me?" All of the signs God had given. He had given them provision, and they had seen that. God had given them protection. They had seen that. He had given them His presence. They had seen that. Every night He gave them the pillar of fire to let them know that in their dark hour He was there. He never left them wandering by day; the cloud was ever present to lead them. When God gave the Israelites the law at Mt. Sinai, the Bible says they heard Him and they saw Him in the cloud.

They saw Him; they heard Him, but they were ready to retreat. They wanted to go gack—to go the other way. Numbers 14:1, "And all the congregation lifted up their voice, and cried; and the people wept that night." A bunch of backsliders' tears! Crying doesn't mean one is right with God. You may be crying because you did not get what you wanted, or because there is too great a price to pay to get your way.

"And all the children of Israel murmured against Moses and against Aaron: and the whole congregation said unto them, Would God that we had died in the land of Egypt! or would God we had died in this wilderness! And wherefore hath the Lord brought us unto this land, to fall by the sword, that our wives and our children should be a prey? were it not better for us to return into Egypt? And they said one to another, [That makes one wonder whether they were Jews or Baptists.]*Let us make a captain, and let us return to Egypt."*

"Let's vote Moses out and get us a new preacher," they were saying. "Let us get us a new captain. Let's retreat. Let's go back in another direction."

You know what happened? They saw the difficulties in the land bigger than the Deliverer of the land. They saw the giants to be greater than God. All of the beauty, glory and provision of that land was hidden. All they could see were giants everywhere. Difficulties! "If we go down by the river, the Amalekites are there. If we go to the mountain, the Jebusites are there."

Wherever they turned, they saw difficulties in the way; so they retreated.

That's what most Christians do. You know your problem today? You see your difficulties bigger than the Deliverer. You see those giants that are out there ahead of you if you attempt to preach, if you attempt to teach, or if you attempt to live right or do right; and you say, "I can't be a Christian in the place where I work, or I won't tackle that bus route, or that Sunday school class. I can't go to the mission field. I won't tackle the ministry." You see nothing but giants out there. You see the difficulties in your life, but you can't see the Deliverer.

Brother, the exciting thing about the Christian life is seeing God kill off giants! Glory to God! Don't you know it was exciting that day when they saw God tear down a wall! Tear it down; sink it into the ground! Why, some of you Christians have not lived godly enough and steadfastly enough or gone forward enough to see that God ever did a mighty thing.

Some of you now have retreated in your Christian life. That is not the way. You have allowed the difficulties in life to keep you from the blessings of God. But the blessings are out there for us! Retreat turns you away from the blessings.

The crossing of the Jordan River and going into Canaan is not a type of going to Heaven. When we sing, "I Won't Have to Cross Jordan Alone," the application is not to dying and going to Heaven. The application is that as you make your decision to believe God, you will enter that land of spiritual blessings that God has for you here in this lifetime.

The Bible says, "Eye hath not seen, nor ear heard, neither have entered into the heart of man, the things which God hath prepared for them that love him." That's not beyond the grave; that's in this lifetime. That's here and now. There are the pomegranates, the figs, the clusters of grapes which are meant for you now in your Christian life. The point is, are you willing to claim them? The Israelites were not willing to possess this land. Instead, they would make them a captain and return to the wilderness.

Is that what you have done in your Christian life? Have you given up? Have you gone back on God?

You gave up the march to that life and that land of blessing that God wants you to have. You have gone back on God. You retreated. You listened to the crowd. You would not listen to those two little old men—those two among two million standing up and saying, "Let's go! Let's go! Let's get it!" All you heard was the murmuring and complaining. You began to visualize all those giants, those difficulties. So, you slipped away and went away from God.

Fight if needs be! Stand if needs be!

Did you read of the incident of Missionary Bitterman who was shot to death in Colombia? Brother John was telling me of 129 other Wycliffe translators and their families who determined to stay in that country. They did not retreat. They took a vote among themselves and said, "We're staying." They put their lives on the line; they put their families on the line, if needs be. They moved forward; they would not retreat.

There's difficulty out there. There's a struggle out there. If you gain new ground, if you enjoy the clusters—the glories of God—if you enjoy the blessings of God in your spiritual life and know untold joy, you must fight some giants for it.

Keep in mind that the children of Israel were right at Canaan, but they turned around and went around and around and around in the wilderness. For the next thirty-nine years they were neither in Egypt nor in Canaan but wandering between the two places. They were wilderness Christians.

Some of you may be wilderness Christians. You are not in Egypt. You have been saved; you have been delivered, but you have never walked by faith. You have never seen what it takes to have a victorious life, and you are not willing to take up the fight or pay the price for it.

IV. THE REGRET

The fourth word to note in this event is regret. Because of Moses' prayer, the Lord would not destroy this people; but he told Moses that every man that was numbered coming out of Egypt would die in the wilderness. God would not let them go in. What a regret! Now, I have not sat down to try to figure up how many died, but it numbered in the thousands. God let their children go in. But only two men who came out of Egypt were allowed to enter the Promised Land—Caleb and Joshua—who had said, "Let's go possess the land."

When Caleb got into the Promised Land, he said, "This mountain is mine." We sing the little chorus, "I Want That Mountain." That was Caleb's mountain. He claimed it for God. Joshua later led the children of these murmuring people into Canaan's land, but everybody else died in the wilderness.

Maybe you have come right up to the place of blessing in your life; but you saw the testing, the difficulties, and the giants. Maybe in your Christian life you have retreated. You said, "I'd like to live for God; I'd like to serve God; I'd like to take that Bible class; I'd like to do this work, but there are too many giants." So you went back down. You are not in Egypt, but neither are you in Canaan. You're just aimlessly wandering around, marking time until somebody buries you. They'll put up a tombstone; and they will have to say, "This Christian man died in the wilderness. He never got across into the victorious life."

The difficulties of life need not cause you to regretfully retreat. You can go forward into the land of blessings that God has for you. You can claim the victories that God has promised.

The following poem is an encouragement to move forward rather than quit:

Don't Quit

When things go wrong, as they sometimes will,
When the road you're trudging seems all uphill,
When the funds are low and the debts are high,
And you want to smile, but you have to sigh,
When care is pressing you down a bit,
Rest if you must, but don't you quit!

Life is queer with its twists and turns,
As every one of us sometimes learns
And many a fellow turns about,
When he might have won had he stuck it out;
Don't give up, though the pace seems slow,
You may succeed with another blow.

Often the goal is nearer than
It seems to a faint and faltering man,
Often the struggler has given up,
When he might have captured the Victor's cup;
And he learned too late, when the night came down,
How close he was to the golden crown.

Success is failure turned inside out,
The silver tint of the clouds of doubt,
And you never can tell how close you are,
It may be near when it seems afar;
So stick to the fight when you're hardest hit—
It's when thing seem worst that you mustn't quit.

—Copied

CHAPTER 11

Stir Up the Gift
of God

"Wherefore I put thee in remembrance that thou stir up the gift of God, which is in thee by the putting on of my hands."—II Tim. 1:6.

"Yea, I think it meet, as long as I am in this tabernacle, to stir you up by putting you in remembrance."—II Pet. 1:13.

"This second epistle, beloved, I now write unto you; in both which I stir up your pure minds by way of remembrance."—II Pet. 3:1.

Most of us have a tendency to become apathetic in every area of our Christian lives. Just because a person is born again does not mean he will automatically live life to its fullest potential. We must realize that the Christian life is not a magic carpet, nor is it a spiritual peak that one reaches which will always exclude the valleys of apathy. The Christian life and its enthusiasm has to be continually nurtured and stirred. Paul and Peter were both writing to "stir up" the believers who had put their faith in the Lord Jesus. This stirring up was to help them avoid apathy.

Apathy, of course, really means a lack of emotion, a lack of interest. It means a lapse into a listless condition. From this listless, drifting condition, Paul said, "I stir you up." Likewise, Peter said, "I stir you up." Actually, they were saying, "Rise up. Revive again those things that you have in Christ."

From this state of apathy our Lord Jesus Christ seeks to continue to stir us. We may call it revival. We may call it a stirring. However, it is the moving of God upon us by His blessed Holy Spirit and by His Word that keeps our lives vibrant. We need enthusiasm, dedication and determination, or else we will slip back into the apathy that Paul and Peter encourage us to avoid.

Furthermore, a great part of the ministry of any preacher is much like the ministries of Paul and Peter, and that was to keep the people of God stirred up. I pray that God will stir us up. I pray that our fires will burn brightly. I pray that our enthusiasm will be stirred. I believe God wants you to be an enthusiastic, shining, vibrant Christian. I pray that God will cause the fires of purpose and enthusiasm to burn in your bones as it did in Jeremiah's.

I pray that God will do that for us here. I pray that God will do that for me. I don't want to be an ordinary preacher. I don't want to be very nice, calm, and collected. I want some fire, enthusiasm and dedication. I don't want to be listless. I don't want to get where I can't say, "Amen!" I don't want to get into such a state of apathy that I can no longer recognize and enjoy the blessings of God.

Unfortunately, many Christians become that way—filled with apathy. But I pray that God will stir us up. I know that He wants to. And I believe that there are some things that we need to ask God to stir within us.

I. MAY THE GIFT OF GOD BE STIRRED

First, you would have to say, in reading II Timothy, that God was saying to us, "Stir up the gift of God that is in you." I pray this morning that God would stir up that gift in us. There will never be a time that I will not need to be stirred. Paul admonished the young preacher boy Timothy to "stir up the gift of God that is in thee."

What is the gift of God? How many of you in this audience today are saved? Raise your hand. All the choir members are saved. The song director is saved. And I notice that most of the congregation are saved. Put your hands down. When you were saved, you received the gift of God. What is the gift of God?

1. SALVATION: The gift of God is salvation. "For God so loved the world, that he gave his only begotten Son. . . ." is God's gift to us. To a lost and dying, Hell-bound world, God's gift—the greatest gift, the most precious gift—is the Lord Jesus Christ. God gave His only begotten Son.

The Bible says in Ephesians, chapter 2, verse 8: "For by grace are ye saved through faith; and that not of yourselves: it is the gift of God." Salvation and Christ: salvation in Christ is the gift of God. I believe, beloved, that God would have the gift stirred within us. Christ in your life should stir you up to be vibrant and afire for Him.

Many have left their new life in Christ. Their new experience in Jesus has slipped away and settled down at the bottom of the sea of apathy, and the waves have rolled over the top. You know what has happened? Somewhere along the line, the joy, the happiness, and the song that you had in Christ and the smile for God upon your face have slipped away. The rejoicing of sins forgiven, the idea of going to church and reading the Bible, the excitement of it all has somehow slipped away from you.

You cannot sing, "He lifted me up out of the miry clay, set my feet upon a solid rock, and put a new song in my heart." The song has gone. The vibrant enthusiasm with which you once sought the Book of God and the worship of God has somehow settled at the bottom of the sea of indifference. Now, in a very listless condition, you need a stirring of the gift of God.

Many Christians today need a new stirring. God, stir up the salvation that we have in Christ. Stir us, Lord, until our light shines. Stir us up until our hearts burn. Stir us up until we cannot contain ourselves. Stir us until we are constrained to let the world know that Jesus has saved us and set us free. Yes, our salvation needs to be stirred up in the Lord.

As the psalmist thought of how sin had robbed him of his joy, on one occasion he sang, "O, he hath lifted me up." And he sang the second verse, "He hath restored my soul." And he sang the third verse, "He hath set my feet on a solid rock." And he sang the fourth verse, "He hath put a new song in my heart, and joy in my soul." However, when reading Psalms 50 and 51, you will find that David let this joy steal away from him. Sin had brought ruin. Sin had taken away his son. Sin had taken away his joy. Sin had taken away everything.

That is the way sin is. Sin will take everything it can take. It will steal your laughter, your fellowship, your rejoicing, your "Amen," your smile. Sin can steal your family. And sin will take the joy from your heart and leave you listless.

I think of how the psalmist prayed, "O, restore unto me the joy of thy salvation." Restore unto me the JOY of it. Not restore salvation, but restore the joy of it. Thank God, we poor mortals cannot lose our salvation! For if we could, we probably would. We would get into sin. We would get away. We would get so backslidden. But, thank God, our salvation, our eternal security is not dependent upon our works but upon His work on Calvary. You can lose everything else but your salvation.

I look upon faces of Christians who look as if there is no joy whatsoever. Talk about Heaven, and there is no rejoicing. Talk about sins forgiven, and there are no smiles. Talk about names written in the Lamb's Book of Life, and there are no "Amens." Sing songs about Jesus, and there are no expressions of happiness. Yes, too many Christians have lost the joy of their salvation.

The psalmist prayed, "Restore unto me the joy. . . ." I think he was saying, "O God, stir up my life that has become apathetic. Stir it up, Lord, stir it up."

I have never talked with a backslider who didn't say that the happiest time of his life was when he was serving the Lord. I am convinced that the best days of a Christian's life are when he is going to church, being faithful, reading his Bible, praying, having fellowship with other Christians and when he is trying to live a clean life.

This morning, if you need a new stirring in your heart, then yield to the Lord and ask Him to restore again the joy that you once had in Christ. He will answer that prayer. Don't you want to be happy again? Don't you want to be able to sing again? Don't you want again the JOY of the Lord in your life?

2. SERVICE CALL: In II Timothy, Paul was not only talking

about stirring up the gift of salvation; but he was talking about stirring up one's call to service as well. He said, "Stir up the gift of God that was given unto thee by the laying on of hands." In other words, the laying on of hands was the verification of the fact that God had called young Timothy to preach. Furthermore, the gifts of God and the callings of God are without repentance. God calls some to be apostles, some to be preachers, some to be teachers, some to be bus captains, some to be Sunday school teachers. But God calls everybody to do something for Him. Everyone has been given a particular job to do for the Lord whether that job be little or big in the eyes of man.

Paul was telling Timothy to stir up the gift of his service. In other words, keep it alive. Be sure to stir up the gift of God that is within you to serve the Lord with enthusiasm and excitement.

Ladies and gentlemen, I'm here to tell you that as a preacher for some twenty years there are times when discouragement comes. There are times when you want to ask, "Lord, is it worth it all?" There are times of defeat and discouragement. As you look back on that time when God called you to preach, you have to find a prayer closet and pray, "O Lord, stir up the gift of preaching again. Stir me up, God!" There comes a time when every bus captain, every Sunday school teacher, and every other person who works for the Lord needs to ask God to stir up his gift of service.

You know what ex-Sunday school teachers are? You know what ex-preachers are? You know what ex-bus captains are? You know what ex-ushers are? You know what ex-workers are? People who didn't get stirred up. People who failed to pray and get stirred back to the job.

I'll guarantee that if you will ask God to stir your heart and give you an enthusiasm to serve Him, He will. When I become discouraged and pray for God to stir me up, He stirs me up and sometimes almost too much. I don't want to become a listless, lifeless, emotionless Christian who just drifts along or who settles down to the bottom of the sea of apathy.

Yes, there will be storms on top, but I want to be where the storms are! On the bottom, one is not bothered by many things, but who wants to be on the bottom all the time! It's silent down there. I want to be where something is going on. God, stir me up! Stir up my service! Set me aflame again!

II. MAY OUR LOVE BE STIRRED

First, our gift ought to be stirred. Second, we ought to pray, "O God, stir our love." When we were first saved, there was a burning, blinding, dedicated love for Jesus in our hearts. Everything else took second place. Christ was first in our lives. But eventually other things began to take first place, and our love for Jesus was gradually pushed into the background. As a result, we have become like those to whom Jesus had John write, "I have somewhat against thee, because thou hast left thy first love. . . thou art neither cold nor hot. . .thou art lukewarm." God would rather have us cold or hot in his mouth than to have us lukewarm. Our love for the Lord Jesus needs to be stirred. It is evident that our love for Jesus and our love for the things of God has cooled off.

Do you love the church as you once did? I know Christians who never missed coming to the house of God, but they miss now.

I know folks who would never let the Bible get away from them, but they don't read it now.

I know folks who at one time were vibrant and glowing, but now their lives seem to be just the opposite; they have cooled off.

Many Christians used to love Jesus and His Word, but now they have let this love get away from them. Our love needs stirring. We need a baptism of love. We need to pray, "Lord, warm up and set on fire my love for Thee." Jesus will answer that prayer.

If your love is stirred up and on fire for God, you will begin to love the things you ought to love and hate the things you ought to hate. God will help you love the right things as your love is stirred up toward God.

Look with me to Ezekiel 33, verse 31:

"And they come unto thee as the people cometh, and they sit before thee as my people, and they hear thy words, but they will

not do them: for with their mouth they shew much love, but their heart goeth after their covetousness."

Do you know that at times in my ministry I have been guilty of the same thing? There have been times, when sitting in church, I have allowed my mind to wander. Times when I sat in church and thought about something else, such as what I was going to do, how I was going to make a dollar, and how I was going to get ahead. Or what I was going to do when church was out. Or what I could have been doing—thinking what I could have been doing that morning had I not been in church. Then, the Holy Spirit would stop me and I would think, *Where in the world is my mind! I have a purpose and reason for being here. Lord, stir up my love for Thee and for the Word.*

III. MAY OUR ZEAL BE STIRRED

We should pray that God will stir up our love for Him, but we also need to pray that God will stir up our zeal. I'm talking about the eagerness, the willingness that God's people must have to do God's work. Surely God never intended us to be anything but zealous, outgoing, adventurous, conquering people.

We have the idea today that to be spiritual means not to sin, or to be spiritual is simply not to open one's mouth but to remain silent. The Bible doesn't teach that kind of Christianity. It says to go out into the highways and hedges and compel them to come in. It says, "Let your light shine." It says, "Let the redeemed of the Lord say so." The Bible also says, "Go ye into all the world, and preach the gospel to every creature." That sounds like an aggressive force to me. That sounds as though God wants us to be zealous.

Where is the zeal and the enthusiasm with which men, women and young people once worked for God?

Where is the enthusiasm with which bus captains used to go out to build their bus routes?

Where is the enthusiasm with which Sunday school teachers used to pray and lament over souls and seek to win them?

Where is the zeal that teachers used to have to build their Sunday school classes?

Where is the zeal of choir members?

Where is the zeal of ushers?

Whatever we do should be done with zeal and not haphazardly.

Turn to Isaiah 32:9. Oh, this is a beautiful passage in the Word of God: "Rise up, ye women that are at ease; hear my voice, ye careless daughters: give ear unto my speech."

Turn also to Isaiah 47:8: "Therefore hear now this, thou that art given to pleasures, that dwellest carelessly, that sayest in thine heart, I am, and none else beside me; I shall not sit as a widow, neither shall I know the loss of children."

Let us not dwell carelessly. Where is thy Holy ambition? Is there no one who wants to be somebody for God? God is looking for a man who wants to do a work for Him. God is looking for a teenager who wants to work for Him. God is looking for people who have enough zeal to get up and go after the things of God, people who want to sing, preach, or teach with enthusiasm and zeal. Where are those who used to go to war but no longer go? They have given up the fight. They have lost their zeal.

Numbers, chapter 32 and verse 6 gives a tremendous challenge: "And Moses said unto the children of Gad and to the children of Reuben, Shall your brethren go to war, and shall ye sit here?"

Think about that. Often there is a need for workers in every church across the land, but the people sit. I am reminded of this passage of Scripture again: "Shall your brethren go to war, and shall ye sit here?" Where is the zeal with which men ought to do the work of God?

As a pastor, it is easy to tell who has and has not the zeal of the Lord. The fellow who has just about lost all his fire will be "dragged down." He has lost his song. He has lost his joy. He knows when the end of the service is near. He can hardly wait to get out. He is saying to himself, *Only two more minutes! Thank God! Praise the Lord!* (That's the only time he prays all week.) If the preacher goes two minutes over the usual closing time, this fellow begins to squirm. *Now, only fifteen more seconds and it will all be over.* But the preacher goes over two minutes, and he groans, *O, no! He's going longer today. He has gone past twelve o'clock already! Maybe he will get it over with in a minute.* He is looking at his watch, shaking it to see if it has stopped. Now he begins to beat on it. *That preacher ought to get himself a calendar instead of a watch. Lord, isn't he ever going to quit?* Then, *Thank God! He has finally quit! Gonna sing. Lord, don't let them sing two verses today. And don't let them get into one of those long, drawn out invitations.*

The congregation begins to sing. They sing two. . .three verses. The preacher says, "Let's sing another."

O no! He's going to sing another one!

Somebody comes forward to the altar. They say, "Let's sing another verse."

The fellow groans. Finally, after about fifteen minutes of invitation, a few folks get saved. Instead of praising the Lord, this fellow says, *Thank God! It is over.* And he goes out.

Another fellow comes to church. He has not lost his joy. He is filled with zeal and enthusiasm. He's been to war. He's been out on a bus route. He's been in a Sunday school class. Boy, he has worked hard, and he has prayed. He has said, *O, God, I need 50 on my bus today. I need 100 on that bus route. God give me a goal in my Sunday school class today. O, God! I pray for those five teenagers in my class who are lost. Please save them.*

As I begin to preach, this zealous fellow sits and prays, *O, God, pour out your Spirit on our preacher today. O, God, let him preach. Lord, speak to hearts today.* About the time I have just one more point, he says, *O, God, don't let him quit with one point. Give him five more points. Help him to preach on because those lost souls have not yet made a decision for Jesus.*

Finally the invitation is given. The concerned Christian prays, *O, Lord, let them go down.* Pretty soon, he sees about five people whom he has invited to church. Two of them come down the aisle. This fellow has a fit: *Oh, praise the Lord! Don't let him quit. Lord, he said he isn't going to sing but one more stanza. Lord, give him five more stanzas. Lord, don't let the choir quit singing. Don't let the music quit. Let them keep singing. I have three more who need to be saved. Let them get saved.*

The preacher says he is going to quit. This is the last stanza. So, this fellow runs down the aisle himself, gets down and prays to keep the invitation open. He prays, *O God, keep on!*

Do you see what a preacher goes through? One fellow is praying that I will quit while the other is praying that I will go on. I don't pay attention to either one of them. I do what I want.

At the end of the service, the zealous Christian prays, *O God, thank you! Lord, I saw five of the people I invited to come to church today get saved.* This fellow walks around with a smile on his face and he is as happy as "all-get-out." You know why? This Christian has been to war. This Christian has been in the prayer closet. This Christian has been out there inviting people to come, and this Christian has prayed that they would be saved.

IV. MAY OUR LIGHT BE STIRRED

You know what? God needs to stir up our zeal and send us to war. A fire has to be stirred sometimes. If you are not careful, a fire will just go out. You have to stir it, work at it. You have to kindle it to keep it going. Often, we think we ought to be quiet and calm, but Jesus said, "Let your light shine."

You say, "Oh, but I don't want others to see what I do." That is the very reason God wants it to shine. Jesus said, "Let your light so shine that others may see your good works and glorify the Father. . . ." Not yourself, but God. It is all right to tell folks that you tithe, that you win souls, that you teach, or whatever. It is all right to let your light shine so God will receive the glory for it.

Jesus asked the question, "Do men take a light or a candle and put it under a bushel and stifle it?" I could preach a long time this morning on that text. There are many lights that do not shine, many a light and many a fire that have been stifled because people have taken the bushel of worldly cares and set it over their light. Many a light does not shine because people have set their light under the bushel of money and greed. What happens when we get busy with the world? The first place to suffer is the house of God.

Loyalty, dedication and service to God are the first things you let get away from you. Many a light does not shine now that once shone for Jesus. The bushel, "Just get ahead in this world," got in the way. Some have let the bushel of fun and worldly pleasures stifle their light.

I say, "O God, let's get the bushels off!"

People ought to get rid of the bushels. They ought to stir up the fire and pray, "Dear Jesus, let my light shine so that others may see my good works and glorify the Father which is in heaven."

If, when you go to war, you go with enthusiasm and dedication, I guarantee you will start getting more out of the victories as they happen. You will rejoice over the folks who get saved and you will be happy.

Keep in mind that some of the greatest Christian services for God were done through lives which were stirred and hearts that were rekindled. As a result, God was able to make new claims on their lives.

Peter's life was stirred again even though he had cursed and denied that he knew the Lord. Jonah ran away from the ministry; but God dealt with him; and as he preached, Nineveh was stirred. Jeremiah had said, "I will make mention of him no more"; yet, Jeremiah had a stirring in his heart; and he continued to be used of God.

God can use your life. Just pray the prayer, "O God, stir me. Stir my life and use me." God will use you.

CHAPTER 12

Christian Service

Take your Bibles and turn to the 4th chapter of the book of Luke, verses 18 and 19. These two verses stress the importance of Christian service being centered upon the Lord Jesus Christ.

Jesus said,

"The Spirit of the Lord is upon me, because he hath anointed me to preach the gospel to the poor; he hath sent me to heal the brokenhearted, to preach deliverance to the captives, and recovering of sight to the blind, to set at liberty them that are bruised, To preach the acceptable year of our Lord."

Later, Jesus made an astounding statement: *"Greater things than these shall ye do."*

Greater than healing the brokenhearted? Greater than preaching deliverance to the captives? Greater than healing the blind? *"Greater things than these shall ye do."* The things that Jesus did while here on earth were wonderful, and we are to be involved in these things. But He tells us that we can do even greater things.

We are saved from Hell by the blood of the Lord Jesus Christ for a purpose. We are saved to serve the Lord Jesus Christ. Every child of God is saved to serve. Jesus spent much of His time teaching and preparing His disciples for Christian service. He taught the disciples what they were to do, how to do it, and He showed them the rejoicing that they could experience if they were faithful in their Christian service. He prepared them before sending them out. Then Jesus said, "As my Father hath sent me, even so, send I you."

In Matthew's Gospel, Jesus said (paraphrased), "As you go out to serve, I send you out as lambs among wolves, as light in darkness, and as water to a dry and thirsty land." In preparing His disciples for Christian service, Jesus also told them that they would not be welcome in every place that they would minister. But He told them to rejoice when persecuted for righteousness' sake.

In John 14:12, Jesus said: "Verily, verily, I say unto you, He that believeth on me, the works that I do shall he do also; and greater works than these shall he do; because I go unto my Father."

Ladies and gentlemen, the secret, the key to Christian service, is found in this verse. No Christian can say, "I can't." Jesus did not put any limitations on this promise. He said, "He that believeth on me. . . ." If you are a believer tonight, then you are saved. Jesus said, "If you believe on me, the works that I do shall ye do also." We are saved to serve. If you have not found your place of service, then seek the Lord. Find out where God wants you to serve and what He wants you to do, then be faithful in it.

I. SEE OUR PATTERN FOR SERVICE

Look again at Luke, chapter 4, verse 18. This verse contains our pattern for Christian service. Notice that Jesus uses the word ME three times. *"The Spirit of the Lord is upon ME, because he hath anointed ME to preach the gospel to the poor; he hath sent ME to heal the brokenhearted. . . ."*

If we are to serve the Lord, we are to be like the Lord Jesus in the way He served. Our lives need to be yielded to Him for service. In addition, what did the Lord say? ". . .the Father hath sent me. . . ." Who had sent Him? The Father.

A. WHAT HE WAS: Since Jesus is our pattern for service, let's discuss three ways that we can be like the Lord Jesus in our service. First, we are to be like Him in what He was. We are to be like Him in what He was before we can be like Him in what He did.

What or who was He? The Bible says that He was the Son of God. As the Son of God, Jesus lived up to His title and His relationship to the Father. He brought no reproach upon the Heavenly Father. He brought no accusation or statement against the kingdom of God and Heaven. The Lord Jesus lived up to every bit of the name that was given to Him.

Now, you and I, too, are the sons of God; so we, too, are to live up to every responsibility and dignity of being His child. If we are to receive rewards, we must bring glory to the Heavenly Father. We should say, as Jesus said, "Thy will be done." May God give us the grace that we might live up to being every bit of the son of God that we need to be because of redemption in Jesus Christ. So many folk fail to be like Him in what He was.

Furthermore, we should be like Jesus in what He was in living holy. Turn to Romans 1:3,4:

"Concerning his Son Jesus Christ our Lord, which was made of the seed of David according to the flesh; And declared to be the Son of God with power, according to the spirit of holiness, by the resurrection from the dead."

Jesus was holy, old-fashioned holy. Turn also to Hebrews 7:26: "For such an high priest became us, who is holy, harmless, undefiled, separate from sinners, and made higher than the heavens. . . ."

Now turn to Hebrews 12:10: "For they verily for a few days chastened us after their own pleasure; but he for our profit, that we might be partakers of his holiness."

Ladies and gentlemen, if you and I accept the pattern of serving the Lord Jesus Christ, if we would be like Him, then we must be partakers of His holiness as well as His salvation. You know what the church of Jesus Christ needs today? Good, old-fashioned holiness. I'm talking about holy living. I'm talking about being clean, being blameless in this old world in the sight of God and men. We have become so scared of holiness that we have ascribed it as a doctrine of the Pentecostals, but holiness is a Bible doctrine, and we should be partakers of His holiness. Before you do anything for Him, you have to be what He wants.

Notice Matthew, chapter 5 and verse 6: "Blessed are they

which do hunger and thirst after righteousness: for they shall be filled."

If a man is unrighteous, if he is clothed with the rags of unrighteousness, it is because he has no hunger in his heart as a child of God to be holy or clean in this world.

Turn, also, to Matthew, chapter 12 and verse 33: "Either make the tree good, and his fruit good; or else make the tree corrupt, and his fruit corrupt: for the tree is known by his fruit."

Ladies, gentlemen, teenagers, young people, God is interested in the fruit of lives. God wants us to be partakers of His holiness that we may live holy, separated, clean, godly lives. He doesn't want us to make excuses for the dance and beer halls, the tobacco, liquor, and everything else that is attached to this world which dishonors Him. When we get back to old-fashioned, holy, godly living and praying, we will get back to the old-time, Holy Ghost power of God. In this generation, it is hard to find a handful of people who are living holy before God. Why, it's no wonder the church cannot get hold of the Holy Spirit power. It is difficult to find holy men who can pray and get the Holy Spirit power of God.

The Bible says in Luke 1: 74,75: "That he would grant unto us, that we being delivered out of the hand of our enemies might serve him without fear, In holiness and righteousness before him, all the days of our life."

Paul said in Romans 12:1: "I beseech you therefore, brethren, by the mercies of God, that ye present your bodies a living sacrifice, holy, acceptable unto God, which is your reasonable service."

Paul says that it is reasonable that a man live holy unto God. Man is not a fanatic—he is not a "nut"—to live holy unto God. He is living a normal Christian life if he lives a holy life. God expects us to live clean, holy, separated lives for Him. The Bible says in I Corinthians 10:21: "Ye cannot drink the cup of the Lord, and the cup of devils: ye cannot be partakers of the Lord's table, and of the table of devils."

In addition, I John 2:15 states: "Love not the world, neither the things that are in the world. If any man love the world, the love of the Father is not in him."

There are some things that you don't have to think twice about to know they are wrong. There are many things in this present world that are wrong for the child of God. The Bible says in II Corinthians 6:14, "Be ye not unequally yoked together with unbelievers. . . ."

The Bible does not say not to love the unbelievers. Jesus loved them. The Bible also says that He gave His back to the smiters. He gave His cheeks to those who plucked out the beard. Jesus loved the sinner. He loves that lost man out there in that bar, but He doesn't want him there. He loves that harlot down on skidrow, but He doesn't want her there. He loves the man who runs that tavern, but He doesn't want him there. Notice the remainder of verse 14: "Be ye not unequally yoked together with unbelievers: for what fellowship hath righteousness with unrighteousness? and what communion hath light with darkness."

What fellowship has righteousness with unrighteousness? When you start fellowshipping with unrighteousness, your fellowship with God will lessen. You start fooling around with the world—you and I know it—your old heart starts getting cold and away from almighty God. You have missed your fellowship with God. You have missed that daily walk and talk with Him. That still, small voice that speaks to your heart stops when you start fellowshipping with the unrighteous.

Similarly, Jesus asked the question, ". . .what communion hath light with darkness?" When we walk in the light as He is in the light, we have fellowship one with another, don't we? But, when we start walking with that crowd that is in darkness, I guarantee you, we lose our communion. What communion hath light with darkness? There is no communion. But, brother, we have holy communion with God when we walk in the light as He is in the light.

Read with me in II Corinthians, chapter 7, verse 1: "Having therefore these promises, dearly beloved, let us cleanse ourselves from all filthiness of the flesh and spirit. . . ."

Some people have a filthy spirit, but God calls upon us to cleanse ourselves. He did not send us into sin. He does not want us to sin. Don't come to me with the attitude, "Oh, if God would only help me. . . ," to excuse your sin. God will help you! There was never a man going down into sin but that, when he cried unto God, God did not help him. There was never a man going wrong who couldn't get hold of God if he prayed. You are not fooling me. You just don't cry aloud unto God. When you get down to business with God, when you get to the place that you earnestly say, "O God, I want victory over sin in my life; give me victory," then God will help you. He is not deaf. I guarantee you, brother, God can see when you mean business. Let's be like Him in His holiness.

B. WHAT HE DID: Not only are we to be like Him in what He was, but we are to be like Him in what He did. What did Jesus do? Turn if you would please to Acts, chapter 10 and verse 38: "How God anointed Jesus of Nazareth with the Holy Ghost and with power: who went about doing good, and healing all that were oppressed of the devil; for God was with him."

Notice that the fact that Jesus healed was not listed first in this verse, but the fact that He went about doing good. In looking at Jesus as our pattern for Christian service, notice that He went about doing good. You and I ought to try to go about doing good. What can you do that is good? Brother, you can work the works of God. You can teach Sunday school classes. You can pass out tracts. You can pray for people. You can get out and help folks whom nobody else cares about. You can do good.

Jesus healed the sick. He saved the lost. He helped those who had needs. He blessed the weak and He cared for others. May God give us Christians who will spend their time doing good and doing it for Jesus' sake.

I believe if you would do good, you should do it in the name of Jesus. Not in the name of some lodge or organization. What good can you do through some lodge or organization that you cannot do through the church and give Jesus the glory for it?

If you put shoes on kids' feet, put them there for Jesus' sake. If you give glasses to some needy person, give the glasses for Jesus' sake. Do what you do for Christ's sake. He went about doing good.

C. WHAT HE SAID: In addition to being like Jesus in what

He was and in what He did, we need to be like Jesus in what He said. Look at John, chapter 8, verse 28: "Then said Jesus unto them, When ye have lifted up the Son of man, then shall ye know that I am he, and that I do nothing of myself. . . ."

Oh, I wish we could get hold of that. In other words, Jesus was saying that He did not say anything or do anything unless it brought glory to His Father in Heaven. He did nothing of Himself or in His own power. Thus He said, "I do nothing of myself. . .but as my Father hath taught me, I speak these things."

May God's people learn to speak the heavenly, biblical language. Church members who tell dirty, off-color jokes, or use profanity should change their language and speak the language of the Book instead. The Bible says that Jesus has lifted us out of the miry clay; He has set our feet on the solid rock and established our goings, and He has put a new song in our hearts. Just as our language as Christians should be different from the world and should be clean, so should our song be different. If you have a new song, you sing new words.

II. SEE OUR PROGRAM FOR SERVICE

Second, Jesus is our program for service. Look back at our text in Luke 4:18 and 19 where Jesus said, ". . .he hath anointed me to preach. . .preach. . .preach." What is the program that Jesus gave for service? Turn to Mark 16:15, "And he said unto them, Go ye into all the world, and preach the gospel to every creature."

The program for service is to preach the Gospel. Preach the Gospel to the red, yellow, black and white. Preach to every creature. Jesus also pointed out five classes of people in the text to whom we should preach the Gospel: the poor, the brokenhearted, the captive, the blind, and the bruised.

I am so alarmed at the carelessness of people today over lost souls. Their greatest need is to have the Gospel preached to them. Our society is cursed with appalling apathy toward the needs of others. Likewise, many times Christians are cursed with apathy toward helping the lost.

Let me share an illustration from the newspaper. A picture from the paper illustrates the news article and shows a lady standing on a great bridge in Portland, Oregon. She is holding onto the arm and hand of her husband who is trying to commit suicide by jumping into the waters. As the wife is holding onto him, she is pleading and crying out, "Help! Help!"

In the same picture is a teenage boy within ten feet of her just riding by on a bicycle. He does nothing to help. In the picture also is a man walking by almost within a hand's reach, but does nothing to help. The next picture shows the husband as he pulls loose, and this news article says that he plunged to his death. The caption under the second picture reads, "And no one helps." Two people who walk by let this man plunge to his death and do nothing to help.

Preachers across this land cry out from the pulpit, "Help! Help! Help!" But church members by the dozens go on their way and care not that souls plunge into Hell. Nobody cares whether they get saved. However, I think it is everybody's job to care. It is everybody's job to pray. It is everybody's concern to get people saved.

In a service that I held in Alabama, a little boy came all the way to the platform while I was giving the invitation and began tugging and pulling on my coattail. I finally had to quit speaking, turn around, and ask, "Son, what is your problem? What do you need?" As I knelt beside him, he said, "Preacher, would you pray for my Paw-paw? He is not a Christian, and he needs to be saved. I can't get him to come to church. Would you pray for my Paw-paw?"

Does anybody care whether that little ragged boy's granddaddy dies and goes to Hell? Does anybody care? Do you care enough for souls to go out of your way to put Jesus and soul winning first in order to get little boys' "paw-paws" into Heaven?

A. POOR: Notice our text: ". . .he hath anointed me to preach the gospel to the poor. . . ." First, Jesus has called me to preach to the bankrupt, the poor. Brother, this old world of sinners is bankrupt. They have no price to bring. But they need to know that they don't need a price, that salvation is free. "For by grace are ye saved through faith; and that not of yourselves: it is the gift of God."

Who cares about the poor? Who cares about the down-and-outers? Who cares whether little boys and girls and moms and dads in those big apartment complexes and houses all across America die and go to Hell? Who cares?

I have baptized many ragged and dirty boys and girls and adults who were perhaps too poor to do any better. But I have often thought, *Glory to God! Jesus has cleansed their souls!* Those little matted, dirty boys and girls coming off the buses—who cares about them? They don't pay the utility bills, but Jesus said, "I preach to the poor. . . ." If Jesus preached to the poor, don't you think we ought to?

Brother, I don't cull anybody when I try to get them saved and into the church. I don't check out their bank account to see if we want them in our membership or not. I want to know if they want to be saved, and I try to get them in.

Our bus captains went out today. Two of our bus captains had over a hundred on their buses. One fellow had 99 on his. I guarantee you that all of those riders were not clean. But somebody cares for them.

It takes a lot of work to get sinners saved. There aren't many who care about the poor. Jesus said He started off with the poor. I just believe somehow that if we start off at the place where Jesus started, we will have better success. Jesus said, ". . .he hath anointed me to preach the gospel to the poor. . . ."

B. BROKENHEARTED: Not only did Jesus preach to the bankrupt, He preached to the brokenhearted. For He said, ". . . he hath sent me to heal the brokenhearted." This old world is brokenhearted. The only balm I know is in Gilead. The only Physician I know that can help them is Jesus.

What a shame that the dear mother in this news article did not know that Jesus could heal her broken heart! A tearful, brokenhearted mother tells of killing her own daughter. She had gone away to college, had gotten into sin, and had become a "hooker"—just a college girl. Her mother brought her home, but she couldn't do anything with her. Mother did not find the solution to the girl's problem. The story states that she asked her daughter to go with her for a drive. She drove her to the outskirts of the city, stopped and pulled out a gun. Telling the story, the mother said, "I must have gone crazy. I couldn't let her go back to the college—back to that sin bin."

"Judy," the mother said, "I can't let you go."

With her mother pointing the gun at her, the daughter cried, "No, Mama! No, Mama!"

But Mother pulled the trigger and killed her daughter.

This lady could have lived in Southwood Apartments. She could have lived near here on Rex Road. This mother was brokenhearted. Jesus said that He came to help the brokenhearted.

As a pastor, much of my time is spent listening to the tearful, sobbing stories of broken homes, or of moms' and dads' problems with their teenagers and many other problems. This is a brokenhearted world.

I say the only answer is Jesus Christ. We ought to be busy about helping the brokenhearted. There should not be a door in this part of the country that you and I have not knocked on. If we know there are troubles and trials behind those doors, let's not avoid them. Let's go after the brokenhearted and help them.

C. CAPTIVE: Jesus said, ". . .he hath sent me to preach deliverance to the captives." Would you like to be free? Glory to God, you can be! Satan cannot get a grip on you that Jesus cannot break. Jesus has sent us to set the captive free.

D. BLIND: I hasten on. He sent us to open the eyes of the blind. Jesus preached to recover the sight of the blind and He gave us that power. The Bible says that the god of this world — Satan—has blinded the eyes of them that believe not lest the light of the glorious Gospel of Christ should shine unto them.

E. BRUISED: Finally, Jesus said, He has sent me to set at liberty them that are bruised: bruised mothers, bruised fathers, bruised children. Oh, this country of ours weeps over fathers, husbands and wives on skid row who are bruised with alcohol. Our young people are bruised with the effects of drugs. This is a bruised generation. But thank God, He can heal the bruised.

III. SEE OUR PERIOD OF SERVICE

What is our period of Christian service? How long do we serve Jesus? Until we are taken Home or until Jesus comes again. Until the heavens open and the Son of God comes with a shout and the voice of the archangel and the trump of God to catch us away to be with Him. That is how long our period of service should last. We cannot afford to quit before then. There is no retirement or tenure of service for the Christian. No time when our service will end. Jesus said to preach the acceptable year of our Lord. And that acceptable year of the Lord is not only the day that Jesus first came but the day when He comes back again. Our work is never done. You may finish a day's work. . .a week's work. . .a lifetime's work with your company, but our Christian service is never over.

Why must we keep working in our Christian service week after week after week? Because the brokenhearted, the bruised, and the bankrupt are still out there; and they will be out there until Jesus comes. I say to you that there is no laying aside of the task. I can't give up preaching. I must keep right on. You, too, have to keep right on teaching, driving that bus, knocking on doors, and praying as long as there is a soul out there to be reached, as long as there is a heart out there that needs encourgagement.

We can't affort to quit. There are too many "paw-paws" out there who are lost. How many boys and girls, how many men and women have come to me through the years and said, "Preacher, pray for my husband. Pray for my daddy to be saved. Pray that my grandpa will get saved. Preacher, pray for my teenagers." Because of them, I can't throw in the towel. I have to keep at it.

Somebody is counting on me. Is someone counting on you? There is too much at stake; therefore, I can't quit.

"Oh," you say, "Preacher, you don't ever get discouraged?" Well, you just don't know about it when I do. "You don't ever have problems?" You just don't know about them. There are times that I need encouragement just like anybody else does.

I have a card written to me by my son that I keep and read often, especially in times of discouragement. I hadn't been in Georgia long when he sent me this nice card. The front reads,

"For a wonderful Dad, Happy Birthday." And on the inside is this little poem:

"For all the loving things you have done in your own special way;
For all the sacrifices you've made from day to day;
Patient counsel, and wise advice;
For faith and trust and love;
May you know all the happiness you're so deserving of."

Then he wrote a little note:

> Dad, I know this is awfully late, but we ran into a few problems. We couldn't do much, but we wanted to send you a little something to show we care. We hope everything is working out all right with the church in Georgia and that you'll be happy there. Just a note to say that you're the best dad in the world.

For that, I can't quit. That boy is counting on me. He needs me. Bless his heart, he may not be all that he wants to be for Jesus, but I can't throw in the towel. I can't quit preaching. I'm not about to give up. Brother, I want some place for him to come back to. He may not have always liked what I've told him to do, but he thinks I'm the best dad in the whole world.

I don't know what year it was that I received a card from my oldest daughter. I guess it was when I needed it most—on Father's Day. The card read:

> Dad, sometimes it might seem to you that I don't love you and know how wonderful a dad you really are because I'm just a daughter and not a son. But to me you're the greatest dad (and with underlined emphasis) and the greatest preacher. And I love you more than I can ever show. Thanks for just being you.

Now, I can't let that daughter down. I can't throw in the towel. I can't afford to quit and lay down the sword. I have to keep right on preaching because somebody is counting on me. Somebody thinks I'm the greatest preacher in the world.

Somebody thinks my wife is the greatest mom in the world. She can't quit. Together we will continue to do the work of the Lord. We have to keep right on going.

Just once in awhile I'll pull out those cards, when it seems nothing else helps, and read that little part down there that says, "You're the greatest preacher in the world." As I read that, I say, *M-m-m-m-m, I think I'll just keep right on preaching!* I can't ever read the card from my son without praying for him and saying, "Son, may God touch your life again. May God use you." And I believe God is going to use him.

The only hope I have that God would answer my prayer is if I keep in the fight, keep on preaching, and winning souls. Quit if you want. Throw in the towel if you want. Quit your bus route. Quit your Sunday school class. Quit going to church and reading your Bible. But I'll tell you what. You may have a kid looking at you, too. You may have somebody counting on you, too. I'll guarantee you that in spite of all the heartache, problems, trials and troubles, one of these days somebody will sit down and write you a card.

When that teenager was going through his problem years and thought you were the worst mom in the world or when that young boy thought you were the strictest parents a boy ever had, you may have become discouraged; and you may be discouraged now; but when they grow up and find that they were wrong and you were right, they will write a card of thanks and appreciation. However, if you throw in the towel, there'll be no cards to read. If you throw in the towel, you will let someone down who was counting on you.

Quitters don't encourage anyone. If your children are straying, you may have to stay on your knees a long time. You may have to spend a lot of lonely nights and shed a lot of lonely tears about that boy or girl; but if you will stay on your knees, stay in the battle, stay true to Jesus, God will honor that prayer.

Let's not quit. Stay in the battle and in the work. Our period of Christian service lasts until Jesus comes again.

IV. SEE OUR POWER FOR SERVICE

What is our power for service? Certainly, that power is the Holy Spirit's power. Jesus told His disciples to tarry in Jerusalem until they were endued with power from on High. After receiving that power, they were to follow the instructions given for service. This power would permeate their ministries. I'll guarantee it is a special anointing, a special power, that drives our bus workers, Sunday school teachers, and others week after week to do their work for the Lord. You may think bus captains feel good every Saturday. They don't. You may think it is easy for them to go out all day Saturday visiting, bringing in boys and girls, moms and dads. You think they feel good. No, they just have a special anointing. They come in here sick at times. They feel bad. They're tired. They would like to be doing something else, just like you. But they have been out in the field helping the brokenhearted and the bruised.

Some of you have no idea what that is all about. Most church members know only about what is preached from the pulpit on Sunday. They don't get firsthand the work in the fields. Brother Roy Keown made a profound statement: "Every one of these church members ought to come out here on Sunday morning and ride these buses and see what the world is really like. See where the buses stop. See where the children come from. See what it takes to get them here."

Many teachers reap the cream off the top. We preachers often reap the cream. We come in and sit and listen and have the joy of seeing these bus children saved and baptized, but we don't see where they come from. We don't see the bruised families nor the broken homes that they come from.

No, church workers don't feel good all the time. Preachers don't feel good all the time. Bus captains don't feel good all the time. But our backs are to the wall. If we save this generation of young people, if we save our kids, we have to mean business in our Christian service for the Lord. We have to quit playing around. The world is going to Hell. The world is lost and we have a job to do. But we cannot do it without the power of God.

V. OUR PRICE FOR SERVICE

Turn with me to Luke, chapter 14. It costs to get people saved. It takes time. It takes dedication. It takes a lot of harassment. I can't begin to tell you what it costs to get sinners saved. There is a price to pay. I thank God for those who are willing to pay the price to get souls saved. I thank God for those who will buy the buses, build the buildings, and whatever needs to be done to get the job done. There is a price. And you don't win trophies of grace without paying a price.

Mark Spitz didn't win all those gold medals without paying a price. Every Olympic gold-medal winner, brass-or silver-medal winner had to pay a price to win. They abstained from things that would hurt their bodies or their athletic ability. They went to bed early when they might have wanted to stay up late. They had to discipline themselves to get the rest they needed instead of frolicking. They spend hours upon hours perfecting their talent or skill in order to win.

Look at Luke, chapter 14 and verse 21:

"So that servant came, and shewed his lord these things. Then the master of the house being angry said to his servant, Go out quickly into the streets and lanes of the city, and bring in hither the poor, and the maimed, and the halt, and the blind."

Most church members sitting in their padded pews today wouldn't want that motley crowd attending their church. But Jesus wanted them and He helped them. He said to go out after them in the lanes and highways, get them and bring them in. But somebody had to pay the price to get them in. It costs something now to reach the brokenhearted, the blind, the lost, and the bruised. There is a price to pay.

When a church loses its vision of reaching the poor, the halt, and the maimed crowd, God will write "Ichabod" over the door. On the other hand, that doesn't mean we are to forget the rich. The fellow who lives in the $100,000 home needs to be saved just as much as that fellow in that old apartment area. God cares about everybody. He wants us to minister to all, to pay the price that has to be paid to reach all for salvation and Heaven.

VI. OUR PRIZE FOR SERVICE

Last, I think our prize for Christian service would have to be, "Well done." Just "well done," would be enough. But there are many prizes, trophies of grace, that you will enjoy for your Christian service. Maybe some man in Heaven will walk up to you and thank you for leading him to the Lord. Maybe some lady will thank you for inviting her to church where she heard the Word and was saved.

I don't think there will be different age groups in Heaven. The Bible says that we will all be like the Lord Jesus; therefore, we will be ageless. But, Mr. Bus Captain, how would you like to have three hundred little boys and girls chasing you down Glory Boulevard, saying, "Thank you for coming to our place and getting us saved"? How would it feel to have some chasing you all over Heaven just to thank you? Oh, to look around and see the many that you had won or had helped to win to Christ!

When the bus captains get through listening to all their kids saying "thank you, " the captains will go over to bus directors and say, "Thank you for helping us. Thank you for showing us how to get out there and get the job done."

Others will go to the youth director and say, "Thank you for showing us how to get folks saved. I got my own little crowd over here. I'm glad you taught me that soul-winning course. I got folks saved." As a result of the soul-winning course, we have young people who have won many to Christ. They have their group waiting for them, too.

Brother Marty, someone may come up to you and say, "Thank you for getting me saved in the clothes closet. I came down to the church to get an old coat and instead, I got a robe of righteousness. I thank you."

That is what it is all about. Christian service is the greatest thing in all this world. Little dirty, ragged kids are out there whom seemingly nobody cares about. I care about them. Do you? We need money for buses, for gas, for the program to get folks saved. It takes a price. I believe that God will bless that program; but we also need those who will pay the price to go out and compel the lost to come into the house of God. We need those who will go out and win others to Christ.

Do you have a crowd waiting for you up in Heaven? Will you have a group to greet you when you get there? Boy, you talk about a reunion! You want to see Jesus, and Mom and Dad and other loved ones. But, those you will be the happiest over seeing are those you won to Christ, those you kept out of Hell, those in Heaven because you told them about Jesus. The greatest trophies of grace, the greatest prize for Pinecrest Baptist Church, will be the folks we have won to Jesus.

For all this, we cannot afford to quit. Though we may have to pay a price to stay in the fight and win the lost, the prize for our Christian service will be worth it all. We can be assured that God will give us His Holy Spirit power to reach those in need of salvation and those who are brokenhearted and bruised. I have people who are depending on me to be faithful. You have people who are depending on you to be faithful. There is too much at stake and the need of this lost and dying world is so great that we must keep on in our Christian service for the Lord.

CHAPTER 13

Simon Peter

Let us look at the life of Simon Peter and take some things out of his life that will be helpful to us.

Peter's life went on a decline, but he came back to do a great job for the Lord and had a great ministry for God. Although there are some black marks upon his life, Peter was a great servant of God. And almost every great servant of God mentioned in the Bible had some marks of failure upon his life. But these men were able to respond to God's correction, come back to the Lord, and go on to serve God.

The aim of this message is to show the human side of serving God, to show that though Christians weaken, God expects them to come back and live for Him.

Most of the great saints of God had times of sin and weakness in their lives. For example, Moses was a great man of God, chosen to lead the children of Israel out of Egyptian bondage. God's hand was upon him in a mighty way, yet Moses was not allowed to cross Jordan and go into the Promised Land. Because of his disobedience, Moses was taken on to be with the Lord; and Joshua stood in his place to lead the children of Israel into the land.

Another example was Abraham whom the Bible calls a "friend of God." God told him to leave his Father's house, follow Him, and He would make of him a great nation. Abram, who became Abraham, did follow the Lord; yet Abraham weakened. He used poor judgment. He actually lied about his wife, referring to her as his sister. In spite of that, the book of Romans describes Abraham as a man who believed God, a man of righteousness who was saved. He was a servant who staggered not at the promises of God.

Although you may have allowed sin to control your life and cause you to stumble along the way, I hope you will take new courage today and see that you can still be used of God. The Lord is not through with you. He wants you to come back to Him.

Read the story of David whom God says was a man after His own heart. Yet most of us are familiar with the sin of David. But David came back to the Lord. He prayed and confessed his sin and said, '. . .my sin is ever before me. Restore unto me the joy of thy salvation. I want the joy of the Lord back in my life again.' David paid dearly for his sin, but he was known as a man after God's own heart.

Thus, throughout the Bible are found great men of God whose lives have been tainted by sin, but who have been forgiven and again blessed.

How would you describe this great character, Simon Peter, a follower of the Lord Jesus, used by God on the day of Pentecost to preach such a powerful message? It would be hard. At times Peter fought for his Lord; at other times, he denied his Lord. One night, Peter boldly pulled the sword out of the scabbard of the Roman soldier, took a swish and cut off the soldier's ear. However, in just a few hours he denied the Lord.

On one occasion, Peter daringly asked Jesus to let him walk on the water. Peter wanted to trust His Lord. He walked on the water. I know he went down, but at least he got on it and walked awhile. That's more than most of us do.

Peter could be challenged and moved. He believed God. He was willing to step out. Peter was an exciting man who made rash statements at times, such as, "I'll never leave you. I'll never forsake you. Jesus, if everybody else turns and leaves you, I'll never forsake you." But he did.

Jesus gave Peter special privileges, along with James and John. On one occasion, Peter, James and John went with the Lord up on the Mount of Transfiguration. There they saw the glory of God. At this gathering Peter said, "O Lord, let us build three tabernacles right here." Peter envisioned a church building program right there. He was saying, "Let's build some things."

Peter was an enthusiastic individual. But I think probably the thing I like most about Simon Peter is that he was a man with whom most of us can identify. We have been rash at times in our statements. There have been times when we have felt like saying, *Lord, we'll walk on water! We'll do it! Lord, we'll stay with you. We'll never forsake you.* We have also been daring at times, but there have been so many times in our lives that we, like Simon Peter, recognize that we have failed and denied the Lord and that we are weak. Yes, I can identify with Simon Peter.

As I look at the life of Peter, I would have you notice four things that are so very important. First, Peter's decision. Second, the decline in his life. Third, Peter's dejection. Last, his dedication, which made the difference in him.

I. PETER'S DECISION

A. FOR SALVATION: Turn to John chapter 1.

"Again the next day after John stood, and two of his disciples; And looking upon Jesus as he walked, he saith, Behold the Lamb of God! And the two disciples heard him speak, and they followed Jesus. Then Jesus turned, and saw them following, and saith unto them, What seek ye? They said unto him, Rabbi, (which is to say, being interpreted, Master,) where dwellest thou? He saith unto them, Come and see. They came and saw where he dwelt, and abode with him that day: for it was about the tenth hour. One of the two which heard John speak, and followed him, was Andrew, Simon Peter's brother. He first findeth his own brother Simon, and saith unto him, We have found the Messias, which is, being interpreted, the Christ. And he brought him to Jesus. And when Jesus beheld him, he said, Thou art Simon the son of Jona: thou shalt be called Cephas, which is by interpretation, A stone."—Vss. 35-42.

Simon Peter's first decision in his relationship with Jesus Christ was to receive Him as his personal Saviour. Not all who come to the Lord Jesus accept Him, but it is a wonderful thing to be introduced to the Lord and be saved.

Simon Peter's brother Andrew heard John the Baptist say that Jesus is the Lamb of God; and Andrew received the Lord Jesus as the Lamb of God, the Saviour. When he found Christ as his own personal Saviour, he immediately went to find his brother Simon to bring him to Jesus. (That's the way it should be. There ought to be rejoicing after salvation and a desire to see others receive Jesus as Saviour, too.) Finding him, Andrew probably said, "Listen, I have found the Messiah. I have found the Lamb of God. Not only have I found Him, but I have received Him, and I want you to come to Jesus, too."

What a beautiful picture to see a person get saved and go immediately to find his dearest loved ones and want them to be saved, also. I think the first evidence of true conversion is a person's wanting to see someone else saved. They go with the joy of the Lord in their life, seeking to bring their loved ones to Christ.

In the future, Simon Peter would be more in the limelight than brother Andrew; but Simon Peter would always remember that Andrew sought him out and brought him to Jesus. The Bible says that Andrew went and found his own brother and brought him to Jesus.

Now you may have to work at it to get your loved ones saved. You may have to go seek them out. You may have to find them in the place where they are and bring them to Christ. But there will be a rejoicing in your heart to know that you have been used of God to bring your loved ones and others to Jesus Christ.

B. FOR SERVICE: The second great decision in the life of Simon Peter was to follow the Lord Jesus Christ. One cannot serve the Lord if he is not following his Lord. When you accept Jesus Christ as your personal Saviour, immediately a relationship is established. You become a child of God. You have a Heavenly Father. Thank God, He is no longer your Judge; He is now your Father! And you are His son. But as many as received him, to them gave he power to become the sons of God," says John 1:12.

I would rather be a son of God than just a church member. I had rather know that my name is written in the Lamb's Book of Life than know it is on the membership roll of Pinecrest Baptist Church. Why? Because His record is true. His record stands and it will never pass away. When a person accepts Jesus as Saviour, a Father-son relationship is established. Now, Jesus said, you can pray, "Our Father which art in Heaven."

Never forget that ever since you were saved, God has been your Father. Then Jesus says you can pray and ask your Heavenly Father for the things you need. At the time of salvation another special relationship is established—fellowship. Right then you are in fellowship with the Lord. Whether that fellowship remains or not is determined by your walk. Look at I John 1:7: "But if we walk in the light, as he is in the light, we have fellowship one with another, and the blood of Jesus Christ his Son cleanseth us from all sin."

We are in Christ and God, and He has sealed us for eternity. Nothing is ever going to change that relationship, but the fellowship can change. Many Christians are out of fellowship with God, which affects their service for God. Their relationship is the same, but the fellowship with God has been broken. Their fellowship also has been broken with their Christian brothers and sisters, because they no longer walk in the light as He is in the light.

Notice that Peter was ready to follow the Lord. Look in Matthew 4:18-20:

"And Jesus, walking by the sea of Galilee, saw two brethren, Simon called Peter, and Andrew his brother, casting a net into the sea: for they were fishers. And he saith unto them, Follow me, and I will make you fishers of men. And they straightway left their nets, and followed him."

Many folks are saved but are not followers of the Lord Jesus Christ. Simon Peter heard the call. Jesus told them to leave their nets, come after Him, and He would make them fishers of men. Jesus came to save men: "The Son of man is come to seek and to save that which was lost."

He called Simon and Andrew to join Him in the great ministry of catching men. Our first aim in service and our main purpose of being left here is to catch men for Jesus Christ.

The Lord said to Simon, "Leave those nets and come after me." And the Bible says Peter left his nets and followed after Jesus."

God was making a promise to Simon Peter. He said (paraphrased), "You follow Me, come after Me, and I'll take your life and make you a fisher of men."

The world's greatest thrill is to know that God can take a poor nobody, a sinner saved by grace who is willing to follow the Lord Jesus Christ, and make that person a fisher of men. It ought to thrill us beyond words to know that you and I can be used of God to set men toward Heaven.

This promise immediately put Peter in the position of having to make a major decision: *Would business, would income, or anything else stand in the way?* He evidently didn't toil long with his decision because the Bible says that they **"straightway"** left their nets and became fishers of men.

Isn't it wonderful when God puts his hand upon a person and he immediately responds to His call? And when you and I follow the Lord with the purpose for which God has called us, our fellowship is going to remain.

The Christian who is trying to win others to Jesus Christ is following the Lord and obeying His command. All those who go on visitation and try to win souls can say, "Amen." A Christian can sing, "Blessed Assurance, Jesus is Mine"; but Christians must let others know that Jesus can be theirs, too. Yes, let us rejoice in our salvation, but let us rejoice also in the fact that God has called us to follow and serve Him.

Simon Peter made a major decision that day to leave his business and follow the Lord. Let me pause long enough to say this: In order to be a soul winner, one does not always have to give up his job or business to go out by faith and work for the Lord. The Bible says that if a man will not work, neither let him eat. A man ought to provide for his family. On the other hand, if the Lord calls you to preach or to go to the mission field, it makes no difference what you have; you will be better off to leave it and follow the Lord, just as Peter did. However, whatever your vocation, you can still be a soul winner.

II. PETER'S DECLINE

Second, I want you to notice Peter's decline. He went through many learning sessions as he followed Christ. He went with the Lord Jesus Christ on door-to-door visitation. He had firsthand instruction on how to win others. He put his life in the hands of the Lord Jesus Christ who tenderly taught and led him in the way. Peter saw many healed and saved.

But there came a decline in Simon Peter's life. Who can say where it first began? I would have to think that it began with small things. Here was a man who had been on the mountain top, who had been allowed to walk on the water, who had even seen the Lord Jesus Christ transfigured; here was a man who had sat at the feet of Jesus, yet his life began to decline. Never think that you are so holy, so righteous, or that you have climbed so high that you can't come down. The Bible says, "Pride goeth before destruction, and a haughty spirit before a fall."

Oh, I don't want Christians to fall. And they don't have to. I don't say that before you can be used of God you have to go to the bottom. But I do say—beware! be careful!

Peter's decline began with small things. Turn with me to Luke, chapter 22. We know that Satan is after us all. We know that Satan was after Simon Peter, and I think he was after Peter's faith to believe the Lord. You know, when you begin to slip, your faith in God begins to weaken. You begin to doubt the Lord's ability to take care of you, to meet your needs, to save your loved ones. When your faith begins to waver, you begin to decline. I think the Lord recognized this in the life of Simon Peter. Look at Luke 22:31: "And the Lord said, Simon, Simon behold, Satan hath desired to have you, that he may sift you as wheat."

In other words, Jesus was saying, "Simon, I know that Satan is after you, but I have prayed for thee, that thy faith fail not."

He knew that there was going to be a testing of Peter's faith.

Why does Satan come at us to test our faith? The Bible says that the just shall live by *faith*. Ladies and gentlemen, faith is our source of survival in this Christian life. We must have faith that God is, that He will take care of us, that He will use us, and that He will save our loved ones. Without faith we are nothing. We have no hope. Faith is our hope. It is our access to the throne of grace. Faith is to believe God. We also need faith that God will send revival and that God will give our church what it needs.

Jesus asked, "When the Son of man cometh, will he find faith on the earth?" Brother, the Devil is after our faith. We live in trying times. We live in a nuclear age, in a time when men have walked on the moon and explored outer space. But on this little planet Earth, we live in an environment of sin. And in this environment of sin, Satan is after our faith to defeat us, to take away our faith to believe that God is still on the throne, and that He still cares. We begin to decline, just as Simon Peter did, when our faith begins to weaken. Many today are weak and unfaithful to God. Why? Because their faith in God has weakened.

Jesus told Peter that Satan desired to sift him as wheat, and that He prayed for him that his faith fail not.

Simon's faith would be tested in Satan's sifter. Do you know what a sifter is? In the old days, when I was growing up, I often watched my grandmother sift flour in an old round sifter which had a little piece of screen wire on the bottom, a little handle on the back and a crank on the side. She would pour flour in that sifter and shake it around until there was nothing left but lumps.

I'm here to tell you that is exactly what Satan wants to do with your life and mine. He wants to sift us until everything good is gone out of us and nothing is left but the lumps, the unusable part. Though sifted, we must not let our faith in God decline. If we do, God cannot use us.

Now, how does one keep his faith? The simplest way is to stay in the Bible, stay close to godly people, and stay close to the church. If you do not stay close to the place where you can pray and be in touch with God, the Devil will take away your faith. You will begin to doubt. You will throw up your hands and quit. You will not pray for that loved one anymore, because you will not believe that God is ever going to save him. Just remember that your loved one can be saved; nothing is impossible with God.

Peter was so confident that his faith in the Lord would not be shaken that even after Jesus told him that Satan would be after him, Peter bragged, "Lord, I am ready to go with thee, both into prison, and to death." But Jesus patiently answered, "I tell thee, Peter, the cock shall not crow this day, before that thou shalt thrice deny that thou knowest me" (Luke 22:33, 34).

How could a man get so backslidden so quickly? How could he get away from the Lord so fast? Peter did not realize how weak he really was. All of us need to recognize the weaknesses in our lives, and we need to look to the Lord for strength to overcome them. After Peter's bold statement, Jesus knowingly said, 'Simon, bless your heart, before that old rooster will let out a crow, you will deny three times that you even know me.' Peter couldn't believe it. Unfortunately, this self-confidence was the beginning of Peter's decline.

Where does decline begin? It can begin when we have more trust in self than in the Lord. This causes a lack of trust in the Lord. This lack of trust in the Lord will, in turn, cause one to stop praying. He will no longer be vigilant in prayer. When he begins to let his prayer life slip away from him, he begins to decline.

Notice again in this same passage, beginning in verse 39:

"And he came out [the Lord Jesus], *and went, as he was wont, to the mount of Olives; and his disciples also followed him. And when he was at the place, he said unto them, Pray that ye enter not into temptation. . .And when he rose up from prayer, and was come to his disciples, he found them sleeping for sorrow, And said unto them, Why sleep ye? rise and pray, lest ye enter into temptation."*

The disciples were sleeping when they ought to have been praying. After praying, the Lord came back to the group of disciples and each time found them sleeping. Maybe it was that somehow Simon Peter, along with the rest of them, began to neglect his prayer life.

Do you pray? Are you so aware of today's temptations and your weakness that you dare not go to that office, meet that woman, that man, or enter into the world, or pass that bar for fear that somehow you might fall? Do you pray, "O God, I have to go out in the world today, so keep me, help me from entering into temptation"? Maybe you are declining because you haven't seen the importance of praying. We ought always to pray more.

Notice the progression of Peter's decline in Luke 22: 54-62.

"Then took they him, and led him, and brought him into the high priest's house. And Peter followed afar off. And when they had kindled a fire in the midst of the hall, and were set down together, Peter sat down among them. But a certain maid beheld him as he sat by the fire, and earnestly looked upon him, and said, This man was also with him. And he denied him, saying, Woman, I know him not. And after a little while another saw him, and said, Thou art also of them. And Peter said, Man, I am not. And about the space of one hour after another confidently affirmed, saying, Of a truth this fellow also was with him: for he is a Galilaean. And Peter said, Man, I know not what thou sayest. And immediately, while he yet spake, the cock crew. And the Lord turned, and looked upon Peter. And Peter remembered the word of the Lord, how he had said unto him, Before the cock crow, thou shalt deny me thrice. And Peter went out, and wept bitterly."

After his prayer life became lax, Peter began following afar off. Next, Peter got into the wrong crowd. It wasn't long before he sat down with this crowd and began warming his hands at their fire. He began to talk their kind of language; he cursed. He even denied ever being with the Lord.

At that point, Peter must have begun to cry inside, realizing he had failed his Lord. Nevertheless, he kept up his pretense and finally said (paraphrased), "I am not one of His. I don't know what you are talking about."

Do you notice how being with the wrong crowd can cause a person to get away from the Lord? If you begin to run with the wrong crowd, it isn't long before you sit down with that crowd.

You begin to warm your hands at the world's fire. You begin to turn away from the fellowship that you so desperately need with other Christian believers. You begin to let your prayer life wane. Then, you become weak and begin to decline further, until you can actually deny the Lord.

Isn't it something that Peter denied the Lord after making the bold statement that he would never leave or forsake Him? Peter was so sure that, though some of the others might forsake the Lord, he would not. Like Peter, I think we sometimes do not recognize just how weak our flesh really is, how totally dependent we are upon the Lord. We fail to realize how important prayer is to our spiritual well-being. We need to heed the words of warning that the Lord gives when He tells us to beware that Satan is after us.

III. PETER'S DEJECTION

Next, we look at Peter's dejection. Surely Peter's heart was heavy over his decline, his going away from the Lord. Remembering that he had boasted that he would go to prison and that he would even die for his Master heightened his disgust and bitterness over his sin. Perhaps his thoughts flashed back to the tender words of Jesus (paraphrased), "Simon, you really don't know what you are saying when you say that you are ready to die for Me. Instead, Peter, before the cock crows this day, you will deny three times that you even know Me." I don't believe the Lord was rebuking Peter here. Rather, the Lord wanted Peter to beware of his spiritual weakness and instability.

Peter was dejected at his failure. The word dejection means heavy heartedness, lowliness, or sorrow for sin. The Bible says that as the cock crew, the Lord turned and looked at Peter. Then, he remembered what the Lord had said would happen. Perhaps Peter could not believe that he had done such a deplorable thing as to deny his Lord. Oh, he was pierced in his heart.

Is it possible for Peter to have denied the Lord and still be saved? Many Christians today have had the same experience of spiritual decline that Peter had. It is a sad thing that many folk who name the name of Christ have watched their lives literally disintegrate. They have quit the church, quit praying, and quit reading their Bible. They have gotten out of fellowship with the Lord and have turned to the wrong crowd. They have denied the Lord and are walking with the world's crowd.

I believe they are saved; I believe that they will go to Heaven, but with regrets and in a backslidden condition. They will go with tears to the judgment seat of Christ. They will lose rewards because they have allowed their spiritual life to decline.

On the other hand, there are people who make a profession of faith in Jesus Christ, who go on to do some spiritual work for Christ; but then they go away, and we never see any more of them. Perhaps many of them were not really saved. The Bible says, 'Many shall say to me in that day, Lord, Lord, have we not done many wonderful things in your name? And I will say unto them I never knew you.'

There are church members throughout the fundamental ranks of Christianity who are working and doing good things, but who are going to Hell. They are lost without God. All they have is their work and effort. There is no real salvation in their lives.

However, this cannot be said of Peter. Although his decline might give some indication that he never really knew the Lord, Peter was saved. Some say a man who really knows the Lord is not going to curse and deny the Lord. But some will. I guess if we could exhibit some of the things that you and I have done, thought, and said since we were saved, none of us would "look" saved either. But Peter was saved; he knew the Lord; salvation was in his heart.

Furthermore, Peter was grieved and broken over his sin. Verse 62 states that Peter went out and wept bitterly. I don't believe that a saved man can get away from God without grieving the Holy Spirit and being grieved himself. When a Christian sins, it bothers him. If conscience alone bothers a man, then surely the Spirit of God is going to convict him of his sin.

I tell you, it takes great courage to weep over sin. It takes courage to say, "Lord, I've followed afar off. My hands have been warmed at the wrong fires."

It takes grace to weep bitterly over one's sins in brokenness before God. Peter wept bitter, shameful, burning tears to God. But, as Peter repented, he began his journey upward and back to the Lord.

The first step on the road from spiritual decline is at an old-fashioned place of prayer, weeping over sins committed. The Lord will forgive and will help you reclaim that testimony that you lost at the world's fire. He will begin to rebuild within you the character that you allowed the Devil to tear down. Then, you can begin to restore your testimony for Jesus.

Would to God that there were more tears by Christians over their sin, failing, faltering and decline. The heartbreak of the ministry is to watch Christians, whose lives continually decline, stay in their backslidden condition without remorse or tears over their sins and failures.

Peter was dejected, but his dejection was the beginning of victory in his own personal life. There has to be sorrow over sin if there is going to be victory. After repenting, there are other steps to be taken in order to rise above the decline and defeat in one's life. Those steps are (1) to return to fellowship with the Lord and (2) to return to service for the Lord.

Sometime between Peter's denial and repentance, he had an encounter with the Lord that helped bring him back to his place of service. Imagine the picture with me. Jesus had been crucified. Discouraged and not knowing where to turn, Peter and some of the other disciples returned to the fishing business. They fished all night and caught nothing. Tired and hungry, they found Jesus waiting for them with plenty of food prepared. Seeing Peter's dejection, the Lord Jesus kindly said to Peter, recorded in John 21:15: "Simon, son of Jonas, lovest thou me more than these?"

Jesus asked Peter the question three times. He wanted to know if Peter loved Him more than the fishing business, or more than anything else in this world. He asked Peter that question because Peter needed to allow Jesus to have priority in his life again.

Before you can ever be in the place of effective service for the Lord, you have to settle the same question, "Is Jesus the most important person in my life?"

Does He have first place in your life? For Peter the sin question had been settled, but now the love question had to be settled. "Peter, do you love me?"

Amid the fear and clamor of the crucifixion, Peter left off following the Lord. He wanted to give up his call to service; he went back to his nets. But, now, as the Master questioned Peter, He tenderly helped him understand that the motivating factor in his service for Him would have to be his love for Him. Once Peter settled the issue of the love question, he was never the same man again. His life had changed.

IV. PETER'S DEDICATION

This brings me to the next point of the message, Peter's dedication. From the time of this encounter with the Lord Jesus, he devoted and dedicated his life to his Lord and allowed Christ to reign supreme in his life. He allowed Jesus to make claims upon his life. Peter would go to jail. He would be beaten even as his Lord was beaten. He would even die the death that he had boasted about earlier but was not quite ready for. I believe when Peter stands before the Lord in Heaven, he will say, "Thank God, I came back and reclaimed my promise that I would go with Thee, that I would die for Thee."

Peter can rejoice in Heaven because he made his promise good and came back to the Lord from the world's camp—from a life of decline. I am glad he did. Peter came back to a life of prayer, back to fellowship with the Lord, back to his place of service. With God's power upon him, he could be mightily used of God.

Acts 1:13 says, "And when they were come in, they went up into an upper room, where abode both Peter, and James."

Peter was there! He was listening to the Lord. He was now obeying. According to Acts, chapter 1, he spent forty wonderful days in camp meeting and Bible conference with the Lord. The Saviour said to him, as He said to others, "Wait, tarry here, until ye be endued with power from on High."

Peter had learned the importance of the words of his Master. This time Peter listened very carefully, not acting in haste.

Remember how Peter had gone to sleep instead of praying?

This time Peter prayed and waited as the Lord instructed. "These all continued with one accord in prayer and supplication" (vs. 14).

Along with the others, Peter prayed. They had a good, old-fashioned prayer meeting. Peter was first to stand up for the work of God, though he had been the one to deny and forsake the Lord earlier. Brother, this time he is not sitting down with the world; he is now standing and letting the world know where he stands. "Peter, standing up with the eleven, lifted up his voice, and said unto them, Ye men of Judaea, and all ye that dwell at Jerusalem, be this known unto you, and hearken to my words" (Acts 2:14).

Peter let that crowd sitting by the fire and everybody in town hear what he had to say. Brother, when Peter got to the platform and started speaking, he spoke. When he was handed the podium, he didn't back off. He kept at it. In Acts 2:22, Peter said, "Ye men of Israel, hear these words; Jesus of Nazareth, a man approved of God among you by miracles and wonders and signs, which God did by him in the midst of you, as ye yourselves also know."

In other words, Peter was saying, "I want everybody to know Him." It mattered not to Peter what others thought of him. The most important thing now was for him to obey the Lord and share His message with others.

It is amazing the change which comes in a man's life when he really gets right with the Lord. Brother, you are not kidding me. You are not fooling me. This half-hearted, drag-around type of Christian service which most church members give leaves much to be desired. Something is not clicking. If a man gets his heart right and his life on fire for God, he will start letting the world know whose side he is on. We won't have to pull it out of him. He will not have to be coaxed. He will be ready to stand up for the work and Word of God.

Church members who stay silently in the background and who will not stand up for the Lord just have not settled the love question. They have not put first things first. Jesus is not the most important person in their lives.

Peter was now the compassionate one. At one time he had

thought only of himself: "Me, die? Go to jail? No! I don't know Him." Peter had been thinking of his own hide. Now, Peter did not count the cost but started thinking about the only One who counts—the Lord Jesus. He began to honor the Lord Jesus.

Do you realize that the only thing that counts is that which honors God? If it takes our hide to honor Him, then let's give our hide. If it takes our lives to honor Him, then let's give our lives. We need to be as compassionate and as concerned for others as was Peter.

Notice Peter's compassion:

"Who seeing Peter and John about to go into the temple asked an alms. And Peter, fastening his eyes upon him with John, said, Look on us. And he gave heed unto them, expecting to receive something of them. Then Peter said, Silver and gold have I none; but such as I have give I thee: In the name of Jesus Christ of Nazareth rise up and walk."—Acts 3:3-6.

And the Bible says the man got up and walked. Instead of forsaking the work of God, Peter was right in the middle of it. Peter, a man who had lost all power and influence, now once again had the power of God upon him.

Every child of God needs to be involved in the work of God. Every child of God ought to want the power of God upon his life. How does one receive that power? Settle the love question and then pray for that power.

Peter was determined to live for the Lord and serve Him. His new dedication sent him to the whipping post. But, to some extent, Peter must have enjoyed it. Every lash he received, he must have said, "Lord, I needed this. I backed out on You. Now, I am getting what You got when they lashed Your back and shed Your blood." Peter was willing to take the stripes or whatever punishment given him. Only one thing mattered and that was to be true to Jesus and love Him supremely. As a result, Peter continued to preach.

Peter and the other apostles were brought before the council and were commanded not to preach again. In fact, they were not to mention the name of Jesus. At one time, Peter might have been silenced, but not now. The love question was settled. Revival burned within. Peter was dead to self and sin. Brother, you can't kill a man who is already dead. Peter boldly answered the commands of the council, "We ought to obey God rather than man." Look at Acts 5:32 and 40:

"We are his witnesses of these things; and so is also the Holy Ghost, whom God hath given to them that obey him. And to him they agreed: and when they had called the apostles, and beaten them, they commanded that they should not speak in the name of Jesus, and let them go."

The Bible says that they departed from the presence of the council rejoicing that they were counted worthy to suffer shame for His name. Then, they preached daily in the Temple and went from house to house. They did not stop preaching; they merely stepped up their efforts.

The world will have a hard time silencing you if you get your life right with God. You will not be muzzled. A man who was once a coward, a quitter, a disloyal follower, is now a man who cannot be stopped. Peter had a new dedication to serve the Lord.

May God do something for us today. I wonder what you would be willing to endure to be true and faithful? What would you sacrifice? What would you suffer? What would it take for you to be a faithful Christian? To be a good bus captain, teacher, preacher, or missionary? What would you be willing to do? What is the price and how far would you be willing to go?

I ask our young people: Would you be different for God? Would you be clean before the Lord? Would you weep over sins and failure? After you have wept and prayed, would you settle the love question with the Saviour? After settling the love question, would you love the Lord enough to pray for the power of God to make a change for Jesus upon this world?

Peter's transformation and dedication caused him to love the Lord so much that he was willing to go to jail and willing to die for Him. History tells us that Peter asked to be crucified upside down because he did not feel worthy to die as Jesus died. Peter has put the world behind him. He no longer is afraid of what men think. Peter would rather let the fishing nets rot than go back to his old business. The gold that his business could bring mattered no more. Jesus was first in Peter's life. Peter was beaten and later crucified because of his dedication.

That is how far we ought to be willing to go. Everyone of us ought to be dedicated to Christ to the point that we would be willing to die for Him if necessary. Isn't it a shame that the dropouts in our churches, and the dropouts in Christian service, are over petty, "little" things? People think more of themselves than they think of God. We have to learn to die to our own feelings the way Peter died to his personal feelings.

Do you love God enough to get your family here on Sunday morning, Sunday night, and Wednesday night? Do you love God enough to do that which is right?

May God help us. I would like for God to give us about a thousand men like Peter—men and women with character, men and women who are willing to do a great work for God. Most of us can identify with Simon Peter in salvation, in surrender to service, and in his decline. But I wonder, can we identify with him in the extent of his dedication?

May our hearts be broken if sin or failure is there. If you are out of service, may your life be reclaimed for His glory. Pray that prayer of repentance and give all to Him who loved you and gave Himself for you.

CHAPTER 14

Dost Thou Retain Thine Integrity?

"Again there was a day when the sons of God came to present themselves before the Lord, and Satan came also among them to present himself before the Lord. And the Lord said unto Satan, From whence comest thou? And Satan answered the Lord, and said, From going to and fro in the earth, and from walking up and down in it. And the Lord said unto Satan, Hast thou considered my servant Job, that there is none like him in the earth, a perfect and an upright man, one that feareth God, and escheweth evil? and still he holdeth fast his integrity, although thou movedst me against him, to destroy him without cause. And Satan answered the Lord, and said, Skin for skin, yea, all that a man hath will he give for his life. But put forth thine hand now, and touch his bone and his flesh, and he will curse thee to thy face. And the Lord said unto Satan, Behold, he is in thine hand; but save his life. So went Satan forth from the presence of the Lord, and smote Job with sore boils from the sole of his foot unto his crown. And he took him a potsherd to scrape himself withal; and he sat down among the ashes. Then said his wife unto him, Dost thou still retain thine integrity? curse God, and die."—Job 2:1-9.

Evidently, verse 8 tells how sore boils may have been cared for at that time since modern medicine was not in use. Job's wife was aware of the pain and suffering that Job was going through. Seeing his suffering, she asked, "Dost thou still retain thine integrity? curse God, and die."

Her question was a challenge to Job. I really don't know that her remark was meant to be sarcastic. I don't know that she meant to belittle him or show forth her own anger. She may have been bitter against the Lord. Or it may have been a kind of challenge to see if Job would curse the Lord or not. She may have been saying, "Go ahead and get it over. Go ahead and die."

The word "integrity" is found four times in the book of Job and each time it is used in relation to Job. It is found twice in chapter 2. Look at verse 3. The Lord spoke of it as he told Satan that Job was a man who eschewed evil and that Job was a man who could be opposed and challenged but who would retain his integrity:

"And the Lord said unto Satan, Hast thou considered my servant Job, that there is none like him in the earth, a perfect and an upright man, one that feareth God, and escheweth evil? and still he holdeth fast his integrity, although thou movedst me against him, to destroy him without cause."

The second time "integrity" is used, it is used by Job's wife: "Dost thou still retain thine integrity?" The word is used again in Job 27:5: "God forbid that I should justify you: till I die I will not remove mine integrity from me."

Job was firm. He said, "I will not give up my integrity." God recognized that Job would remain true to Him. Job's wife realized Job's determination and questioned whether he would change his mind. But Job realized that what he had was worth far too much to give up.

The fourth time "integrity" is used is in Job 31:6: "Let me be weighed in an even balance, that God may know mine integrity."

Right in the midst of Job's trials and sufferings, which became increasingly worse, Job said to his accusers, "I'll not give up mine integrity. Let me be weighed in an even balance that God may know mine integrity."

Evidently integrity is one of the most important qualities that a man can have, for God recognized Job for his integrity. Furthermore, God told Satan, ". . .he holdeth fast his integrity, although thou movedst me against him, to destroy him. . . ."

What is integrity then? Integrity simply means uprightness, completeness. It comes from the word, and has the same meaning as, perfect—not in the sense of sinless perfection, but in the sense of completeness. Job was a man who was upright. He loved God. He hated evil. He was a man who prayed. He walked straight and did not question God. He was every bit a complete Christian. God saw and appreciated this about him. Job's integrity pleased God.

God describes Job as a perfect and upright man in Job 1:1: "There was a man in the land of Uz, whose name was Job; and that man was perfect and upright, and one that feared God, and eschewed evil."

Here was a man who hated evil but loved God. Here was a man who feared God out of love and respect. Here was a man who walked in righteousness.

How does integrity apply to us as Christians today? Integrity means that dedicated, clean, separated, righteous, holy living that we are to have in our Christian lives. God said that Job would not give up his integrity. Oh, for a man like Job, who realizes the preciousness of his integrity in the sight of God and will not let go of it!

Thank God for the man who won't let the world entice him into giving up his uprightness, his walk with God, his hating of evil, and his love for God. Job was upright in all areas of his life. He was steadfast. He wanted to do God's will. His life was honest and sincere; not hypocritical.

I. JOB'S INTEGRITY

"And the Lord said unto Satan, Whence comest thou? Then Satan answered the Lord, and said, From going to and fro in the earth, and from walking up and down in it."—Job 1:7.

The Lord went on to ask Satan in his going to and fro in the earth if he had considered His servant Job. The Lord described

Job as being perfect and upright and said that there was none like him in the earth. There may have been other good men on the earth at that time, but it is interesting that the Lord said that there was none else like Job. There was a time when God sought for a man who would stand in the gap and fill up the hedge, but the Bible says that He found none. Maybe Job happened to be the only upright man at that time, the only man who walked straight and forward in his day. At least, Job had integrity and felt it worth keeping.

Joshua 1:8 says:

"This book of the law shall not depart out of thy mouth; but thou shalt meditate therein day and night, that thou mayest observe to do according to all that is written therein: for then thou shalt make thy way prosperous, and then thou shalt have good success."

Maybe Job had gotten hold of that very thing: if he took the Word of God, put it in his heart, and walked straight in the eyes of the Lord, he would be a perfect and upright man who pleased God. Job feared and worshipped God and he loved and prayed for his family. Look at Job 1:5:

"It was so, when the days of their feasting were gone about, that Job sent and sanctified them, and rose up early in the morning, and offered burnt-offerings according to the number of them all [This verse is talking about Job's family]:*for Job said, It may be that my sons have sinned, and cursed God in their hearts. Thus did Job continually."*

If you will notice, Job was more concerned about grace for his children than about gold in his house. The Bible says that Job prayed for his family. He wanted to do that which was right in the sight of God regarding his spiritual responsiblity for his family "continually."

A. HIS VALUE OF INTEGRITY: Let's look a bit at how Job valued his integrity. Turn to Job chapter 27, verses 1-5:

"Moreover Job continued his parable, and said, As God liveth, who hath taken away my judgment; and the Almighty, who hath

vexed my soul; All the while my breath is in me, and the spirit of God is in my nostrils; My lips shall not speak wickedness, nor my tongue utter deceit. God forbid that I should justify you: till I die I will not remove mine integrity from me.

Now turn to Job 31: 4-6:

"Doth not he see my ways, and count all my steps? If I have walked with vanity, or if my foot hath hasted to deceit; Let me be weighed in an even balance, that God may know mine integrity."

Move down to verses 10 and 11:

"Then let my wife grind unto another, and let others bow down upon her. For this is an heinous crime; yea, it is an iniquity to be punished by the judges."

Job was saying that if he was wrong and if his heart was not right, then let his wife be turned over to another. He was willing to be judged before God since He knew the very intent of his heart.

How valuable is your walk with the Lord? What are you willing to give up for it? Job retained his integrity and his walk with God under the most horrible of circumstances. What were some of those circumstances?

Job's suffering was so great that he cursed the day that he was born. Job did not curse in the sense of using profanity, nor did he curse God; but he simply cursed the day that he was born. Look at Job 3:1-3:

"After this opened Job his mouth, and cursed his day. And Job spake, and said, Let the day perish wherein I was born, and the night in which it was said, There is a man child conceived."

B. RETAINING HIS INTEGRITY: So awful was Job's torment and testing that he wished he had not been born. His heart was broken over the death and loss of his loved ones. His own health was broken. In addition, no one tried to comfort Job. No one had a kind word of encouragement for him. Yet Job said, "I'll not give up mine integrity—my uprightness."

Job stated in chapter 19, verses 13-17:

"He hath put my brethren far from me, and mine acquaintance are verily estranged from me. My kinsfolk have failed, and my familiar friends have forgotten me. They that dwell in mine house, and my maids, count me for a stranger: I am an alien in their sight. I called my servant, and he gave me no answer; I intreated him with my mouth. My breath is strange to my wife, though I entreated for the children's sake of mine own body."

Even for the sake of Job's children, his wife would not reach out a hand of understanding and comfort. None of Job's household would comfort him in this dark hour of sorrow and despair. Still Job valued his stand for God, his integrity, his doing right.

Look at verses 18 through 22 of this same chapter:

"Yea, young children despised me; I arose, and they spake against me. All my inward friends abhorred me: and they whom I loved are turned against me. My bone cleaveth to my skin and to my flesh, and I am escaped with the skin of my teeth. Have pity upon me, have pity upon me, O ye my friends; for the hand of God hath touched me. Why do you persecute me as God, and are not satisfied with my flesh?"

Job had become the laughingstock of the country. Even the children, the young kids, jeered at him. Everybody was saying, "Here is a man who has sinned in his closet. God has sent down judgment upon Job!" Everybody—his family, his friends, his maids, his servants, his wife, the little children—all scoffed at him.

With his flesh rotting, Job was covered from one end of his body to the other with running sores. Job, chapter 7, states that the worms and maggots were in his flesh. In this horrible circumstance, Job said to those about him, "Isn't it enough to you that you see my flesh is gone? Will you take away every kind word? Will you show me no kindness of friendship?" Though no one responded to this plea, Job did not change his mind; he retained his integrity. Through it all, Job kept his testimony of being a man who loved God. When his worldly goods, his children, and everything else were taken from him, Job 1:20 states: "Then Job arose, and rent his mantle, and shaved his head, and fell down upon the ground, and worshipped."

How easy is it for you to give up your testimony and your stand for the Lord? I wonder how many of you would be back in church next Sunday morning if you lost your job? if one of your children died? if your house burned to the ground? or if every friend you have scoffed and laughed at you? If any or all of this happened to you and no one offered a word of comfort, how many of you would be back next week, praising God and saying, "Glory to God in the highest!"?

I am amazed at how easily people will give up their walk with the Lord. Why, there are some who have quit going to church because they didn't get a handshake on a Sunday morning. Others have quit because no one spoke to them. Because somebody slighted them in some way, they quit church and the Lord altogether.

Job wanted his testimony preserved. He wanted others to know how he felt when everyone turned against him and when the children jeered at him. Now look in Job 19:23-27:

"Oh that my words were now written! oh that they were printed in a book! That they were graven with an iron pen and lead in the rock for ever! For I know that my redeemer liveth, and that he shall stand at the latter day upon the earth: And though after my skin worms destroy this body, yet in my flesh shall I see God: Whom I shall see for myself, and mine eyes shall behold, and not another, though my reins be consumed within me."

Job wanted the account of what happened to him put in a book so it would be forever known that he held his testimony. God granted him that request.

When we stand at the judgment seat of Christ, I wonder what will be said of us? What made us quit? What made us throw in the towel? Though the pressuring circumstances of life may overwhelm us, we should not quit. Absolutely nothing should make you quit or give up your integrity.

II. THE ALL-IMPORTANT QUESTION

The all-important question is: "Dost thou retain thine integrity?" Do you have a moral or Christian uprightness about you? Do you have salvation that you can rejoice in today? Do you have a testimony? Do you have something of spiritual value in your life? Is there moral and spiritual uprightness in your life? If so, will you retain it? Will you cherish it? Will you hold on to it until the day you die?

If you die, die with uprightness. You may not be rich, but you can die with integrity. You may not die with popularity, but you can die with integrity. You may not die with the greatest things that this world can offer, but you can die with integrity. You can maintain your Christian living.

Unfortunately, some have given up their integrity already, as Esau did for a mess of pottage. You know the story found in the book of Genesis, chapter 25. Jacob and Esau were twins. Esau was the firstborn and, therefore, was to receive the birthright. The birthright was of great importance. Look in Genesis 25, verses 29, 30:

"And Jacob sod pottage: and Esau came from the field, and he was faint: And Esau said to Jacob, Feed me, I pray thee, with that same red pottage; for I am faint: therefore was his name called Edom."

Seeing this as an opportunity to bargain with Esau to get that which he coveted, Jacob said (paraphrased), "I'll make a bargain with you. Let me make a deal with you."

Esau said, "What is the deal?"

Said Jacob, "Sell me this day thy birthright for this mess of pottage. Let's trade."

Esau said, "Behold, I am about to die; and what profit shall this birthright be to me if I'm dead?"

So they traded. This one little insignificant meal, this one little pot of pottage, was more important to Esau than his birthright. Esau said he was about to die, that he could not live without the pottage. Now you know he wasn't about to die. Unlike Job, Esau was healthy. He was in the land of his friends, his family. He was talking to his brother. He had no reason to sell out.

Some Christians are like Esau. If they don't get that automobile, that other house, that other big room, that next thousand dollars, they think they will die. They won't. Most of the time our wants become more than our needs. We are living in an age of greediness.

Esau said, "All right, it's a deal."

And Jacob said, "All right!"

Genesis 25:33,34:

"And Jacob said, Swear to me this day; and he sware unto him: and he sold his birthright unto Jacob. Then Jacob gave Esau bread and pottage of lentiles; and he did eat and drink, and rose up, and went his way: thus Esau despised his birthright."

The birthright was for the firstborn and meant that he would have dominion over the servants and over other members of the family. He would be number one. The birthright meant that after his father died, he would receive a double portion of the inheritance. According to Romans 8:29, the firstborn was a type of the Lord Jesus Christ Himself, who was the firstborn from the dead.

Today, too many of God's children have sacrificed the benefits and blessings of their Christian lives for a mess of this world's pottage. For some little something to quickly satisfy the flesh and make the flesh happy, they have sold out to this world, the flesh and the Devil. We have the idea today that we should eat, drink and be merry, and do what we want without regard for the consequences. Whatever the price we have to pay for it, satisfying our own fleshly hungers has become the most important thing in our lives. If it means giving up our Christian testimony, giving up the things of God which are important, or giving up church, then the attitude is, "Let's give it up!"

We think we have to have these pleasures or we will die. You're not going to die from not giving the flesh what it wants. Your life for Jesus Christ ought to be worth far more than any weekend on the lake without God. Your uprightness is far more important than a mess of this world's pottage. Your integrity is far more important than a few brief moments in the pleasure of sin. Furthermore, your testimony is more important than putting your own selfish desires ahead of the Lord.

Personally, I like sports. I like football. I never played football because I was always scared I would hurt somebody. . .mostly myself! I didn't want to get into something like that. I just don't have the killer instinct. I like golf, though, and I don't mind hurting an ant if he gets on my ball. However, as much as I like sports, I would not give up my integrity for golf or football or anything else.

Unfortunately, many Christians in fundamental churches do not have a good testimony because they have sacrificed their integrity for what this old world has to offer. They excuse themselves by saying, "Man, I have to have fun. I have to have some time for myself. I have to enjoy myself sometime." Tertullian, one of the great Christians of the past, said, "There is only one 'must' in my life and that 'must' is that I must be true to Jesus Christ who loved me and gave Himself for me!" That ought to be the "must" in our lives, too. We need to retain our integrity, our uprightness, and walk straight forward for the Lord and not turn to the right nor to the left.

Regrettably, there are some Christians who are no longer used of God as they once were. You and I know that there are preachers, deacons, evangelists and church members who are sitting idle in the ashes of sorrow because they sacrificed their integrity. Some gave up their integrity for the desires of lust, sin and sex. I pray that somehow you will realize, as Job did, that your integrity, purity and walk with God are worth far more than any "thrill."

Young person, the keeping of your purity is far more important than any fling with a girl or boy in a parked car or motel room. Many a girl who used to be pure is not pure any more. Many a boy who used to be clean is not clean anymore. Like Samson, they have given in to the lustful desires of the flesh and have lost their testimony for Christ. They can no longer witness and win others to Jesus Christ because of the sin that stands between them and the Holy Spirit's power.

I know Christian men who say that they are saved, and they

belong to the church, but they operate their business as crooked as a snake. How often can the unsaved say, "Man, if you want to do business, don't go to that place. That fellow claims to be a Christian, but he is crooked!" These Christian men have sold their testimony to get ahead in this world.

Listen! It is better that you die with integrity and no money in the bank, than to die with a lot of money in the bank and no integrity.

Do you remember what Solomon said? He said (paraphrased), "I got me women. I got me silver and gold. I got me houses and lands. I built vineyards. I have everything that my heart could desire or want. But vanity of vanities—all is vanity."

This old world system is going to run out on you one of these days. Money will not satisfy and many will do what others have done who had great wealth but did not know what to do with it. Since it did not satisfy, they blew their brains out.

The thing that is most important is keeping one's integrity. I may not pastor the largest church in the world; I may not own the biggest automobile, and I certainly will not have the most money in the world; but my uprightness and integrity with my brothers and sisters in Jesus Christ is worth more than anything else.

Joseph was an example of one who kept his integrity rather than give in to the lust of the flesh. After Joseph had been brought into Potiphar's house, Potiphar's wife laid her eyes on this fine, big, healthy, young man. When her husband was away, she tried to entice Joseph; but Joseph would not give up his integrity for that. She may have said, ". . .but everybody is doing it." Joseph said, "No, everybody is not doing it. I'm not doing it!"

Thank God for some who will stand firm and hold on to righteousness, purity and godliness! Some people are still straight.

The next time Potiphar's wife came sashaying through the house, she ran up to Joseph, got hold of him and said (paraphrased), "Say, Joseph, this would be a good time. Potiphar is away on business." She grabbed Joseph's coat. She had him by the coattail, but he just slipped out of his coat and took off. Joseph suffered for that, but it was worth it. Potiphar believed the lie she told on him. God allowed Joseph to be sent to prison. Joseph was removed from his position in Potiphar's house. But Joseph would rather be in prison facing death than give up his uprightness in the eyes of God. It's better not to have a coat; it is better not to have a lucrative position, yet have righteousness and integrity.

God have mercy! What in the world is the matter with us today? We will sell out God for another dollar, for another house, for another weekend. We will lose our uprightness and testimony for almost anything that comes along. God give us some men and women in this generation who will walk straight and live for God. Some have given up their integrity in times of trouble and sorrow, instead of taking Job's attitude found in Job 23:10, "But he knoweth the way that I take: when he hath tried me, I shall come forth as gold."

Job's wife said, "Job, dost thou retain thine integrity? Why don't you curse God and die?" Job answered, "No, I cannot do that. I cannot curse God. I cannot and I will not give up mine integrity. Though the worms eat my flesh before my eyes, yet, I'll trust God."

The Bible says that the latter end of Job was better than the beginning. God blessed Job for his determination to hold on to his integrity. Please know that every life is going to be tried and tested. The following illustration taken from the "Daily Bread" compares the testing of metals with the testings which our omnipotent Lord will allow us to have in His design and purpose for our lives:

"During the Second World War, I worked as a metallurgist. It was my duty to test the steel being used to build tanks for our boys on the front lines. We had to be sure that the metal was not too hard or too soft as it passed through the tempering furnaces. Tension was applied to ascertain its breaking point. Checks were also taken to make certain that the armor would be bulletproof. If any flaws showed up in the steel, it would undergo more tempering. Thus when it left the factory, it was fully prepared to withstand the stress demanded of it.

"So it is with God's children. To make us fit for His work and the instruments of His praise, He puts us through the kiln of trial and places us in the testing room of life. Pressures are constantly applied to sanctify us and to reveal the weaknesses which only His grace can remedy."

CHAPTER 15

My Testimony

"Hast thou not known? hast thou not heard, that the everlasting God, the Lord, the Creator of the ends of the earth, fainteth not, neither is weary? there is no searching of his understanding. He giveth power to the faint; and to them that have no might, he increaseth strength. Even the youths shall faint and be weary, and the young men shall utterly fall: But they that wait upon the Lord shall renew their strength; they shall mount up with wings as eagles; they shall run, and not be weary; and they shall walk, and not faint."—Isa. 40:28-31.

Whenever I sign anyone's Bible, I always write Isaiah 40:31 along with my signature. I don't know how verse 31 came to be my life's verse, but it has been for some time.

Now along with this text, let's also read Ephesians 2: 8, "For by grace are ye saved through faith; and that not of yourselves: it is the gift of God."

This scripture was quoted to me on the day of my salvation, which did not come as early in life as I wish it had.

In my early years, I had no thoughts of Christ, no thoughts of Christianity, no thoughts of being saved. Church did not interest me. As a young boy, I went to church and Sunday school very little. Probably the longest that I attended at any one time was, I think, twelve weeks to win a zippered Bible in Sunday school. I really didn't care—didn't want a Bible necessarily. But the idea of getting something attracted me. And as a kid, I walked to a little community church for twelve Sundays without missing a

Sunday, in order to win a Bible, a Bible that I never read, a Bible that I could not to this day tell you what happened to it.

Church was something out of the question in my life. I remember going to a Seventh-Day Adventist church three times, a Methodist church a few times, and a Church of God once.

Attending the Church of God was an unforgettable experience. They scared me so badly, I never went back there. The preacher got up and ran back and forth across the platform and preached hard on Hell. I mean he preached it straight, and he preached it hot. The more he preached about Hell, the more I determined that if I ever got out of that place, I'd never go back again. I don't remember how I got to that church. I was just a little fellow sitting on a pew. I could just see the preacher over the top of the pew. I'm telling you, he had me spellbound! He scared me to death as he preached on Hell.

As I look back and see myself sitting there on that pew, I remember thinking, *If I ever become a preacher, Hell is what I'm going to preach on. That really gets to them. That really scares them!* I never did go back to that church.

I went to a Methodist church a few times. I decided that was the church to attend, if I wanted to go to church. This particular Methodist church had dancing parties and a lot of activities that just suited this unsaved young fellow. I said that if I ever joined a church, that would be the one. But I didn't.

My father was an alcoholic, the kind that could stay on the job and work. He was rather faithful about working in his late twenties and early thirties. We had a good automobile in those days. I can remember that we always had nice clothes and nice things. But, when I was ten years old, my father died. Alcohol had taken his life.

After that, things began to go downhill for our family. My mother went to work. We had to move in with our grandmother, who lived alone. Then, we knew what poverty and being poor was really like. We had to go without a number of things. I can remember going through grammar school without wearing shoes. I can remember having iced tea as a treat and only on Sundays. That was a big day to have iced tea. I remember eating a lot of hoe-cake and flour gravy. My grandmother would take flour and make hoe-cakes in the frying pan. Then she would take a little water and mix it with the flour and make gravy out of that. Then, we would pour the flour gravy over the hoe-cake and eat that as breakfast before going to school

As a young boy, I pretty well did as I pleased. I didn't get better. I didn't get closer to God. No one in my family was saved except the godly grandmother on my mother's side. But, we never went to church.

I can remember starting to get into trouble as an eleven-and twelve-year-old-boy. At the age of thirteen, I was already in serious trouble with the law. I had already begun to go downtown and steal things that I didn't have. Some of us boys would go into town with enough money to go to the show, then we would steal mints, chewing gum, candy. . .before long, we decided we would try to do a little better and move up to "big time."

Three or four of us got together one night and decided to break into one of the local stores. We broke into the store through the back. We took all the money from the cash register and started to leave. We were still kids enough to want to fill our pockets with little five-cent cakes that could be bought then, and candy. Everyone had filled their pockets and had left except me. I was a little more greedy than the rest. I was still stuffing cakes into my pockets as I came out the back window which was on top of a shed. Coming out and looking down, I looked right into the beams of a great big flashlight put into my face. A voice on the other end bellowed, "Boy, what are you doing up there?"

Bless his heart, I hit him right in the face with three of those cakes just as hard as I could, and I mean, I took off running! I never ran so fast in all my life. The man knew me. He lived next door. He had seen me. He knew who I was. I couldn't tell what he looked like in the dark. I just hit him in the face and took off. I ran and ran and ran and ran. I ran home. I ran into the house. My grandmother asked if I wanted something to eat. I said that I was not hungry. I ran into the bedroom and said, "I'm going to bed."

My grandmother said, "Gracious day! It's not even 10 o'clock!"

I said, "Well, I feel awfully sleepy." In the bedroom, I took all the money and stuff out of my pockets and hid it away. I turned out the light and went to bed.

It was not long before there was a knock at the door. It was the police. Boy, they caught us in a hurry. They took us down, stood us before the judge, and the judge paroled us. Though we had stolen quite a bit of stuff, he put us on probation for four years. For four years, I had to check in and was checked on until I was about sixteen.

At sixteen, I went to work for the railroad. At seventeen, I went into the service. I came out unsaved. I went back to my job with Seaboard Railroad in Florida. It was there that I was saved. I am preaching the Gospel now because somebody took a personal interest in me. A Christian there cared enough to help me personally. This man was a deacon in a Baptist church and he lived for Jesus every day. As far as I know, that deacon is still living today in Tampa. Every once in a while I can get him to come to my church and I can tell my people, "I want you to see and meet the man who led me to the Lord. I am saved because this man was a soul winner and a good Christian. This man lived for Jesus."

I am reminded of the fellow who said that Gypsy Smith led him to the Lord. He was saved in one of Gypsy Smith's meetings. The fellow took the decision slip which had been made out, took it home and put it on the mantel. Every time he would go into the room, he would salute.

I feel like saluting every time I see this dear man of God who led me to the Lord. I want to salute him for Jesus' sake. I appreciate his leading me to Jesus Christ.

I. I EXPERIENCED MY FIRST MIRACLE

Taking a personal interest in me, this deacon began to deal with me about my need of Christ. I was married. My wife and I had one little girl. I had my life ahead of me. I said, "Listen, I am not interested in being saved." I asked, "You want to go fishing with me tonight?"

He said, "No, tonight is Wednesday night and I am going to church." He continued, "Will you come and go with me to church Sunday?"

I said, "No, man, I'm going fishing Sunday. I can't go to church. Gracious, I got too much to do on Sunday!"

He said, "Ray, you better come on and get saved. You better go to church."

I said, "No." And I would tease him, but I loved and respected him.

You know, though you do not believe and though you do not accept Christ, you have to admire and appreciate somebody who lives for Christ, someone who has a clean testimony and who is trying to help you, someone who is interested in your salvation. You have to care for someone like that. And I did. This deacon never gave up. It was every day, every day, every day.

If this deacon was not after me, a little Baptist preacher, who used to come to the railroad and preach, was after me about being saved. Every Tuesday, every week, this preacher would come out and preach to the guys in the railroad shops. For about ten years, as I worked as a journeyman, finished my trade and worked in the freight yards, the deacon and the Baptist preacher were after me.

I used to play pinochle and horse shoes every day at noon. We would eat quickly and play our games, but every Tuesday, that preacher would interrupt our playing. Well, I mean, I wasn't so bad off that I could play pinochle while a guy was preaching. But I didn't like him at all. I just didn't like his coming out there and preaching. I would complain, "Why doesn't he take that stuff and go somewhere else?" I wouldn't listen. I would go over and lie down and try to sleep. I did not like his preaching, and I wanted him to go some place else, but God worked in my heart in spite of my feelings.

You know, after I was saved and was called to preach, God had me go right back to that same place, stand in those same shops and preach to those same men.

The dear deacon kept working with me. He kept talking to me about Jesus. We were under a freight car one day rebuilding a wrecked car. We had stopped for a minute and were sitting there talking. He took out his New Testament—again. He would get me every chance he could. He read from the Scripture, "For by grace are ye saved through faith; and that not of yourselves: it is the gift of God." I do not know why things were different that day. . .outside the Spirit of God, but I said to him, "Do you really mean that God would save just anybody?"

"Yes, He sure would."

"Do you mean to tell me that Jesus would save, really save me if I received Him as my Saviour? Do you mean He would really do that? Right here with my work clothes on, under this freight car?"

"Raymond, you surely could get saved."

And there under that freight car I trusted the Lord Jesus as my Saviour. Now do not depend upon the feelings that I describe next to be the "results" of your salvation.

When I came out from under that freight car and stood there, it seemed to me that all Heaven lit up. I mean, it seemed as though everything was aglow. Everything seemed changed. I'm telling you, it seemed that I had experienced something unbelievable. I said to the deacon, "I'll go to church with you tonight."

"But there's no church tonight."

"What? Why not?"

"Well, it's Thursday. We have church during the week only on Wednesday night. But, you can come Sunday."

"I'll be there."

My wife was unsaved. We were not drunkards. Saturday night was our night. We would dance and drink and generally have a good time, then go home.

That day I thought, *I can hardly wait to get home and tell my wife that we are going to church on Sunday!* I just knew that she would be thrilled to death. Boy! I ran into the house that afternoon from work and said, "Honey, guess what! We are going to church this Sunday!"

Well, she expected to hear anything in the world from me but that. "We're what?"

"We're going to take Linda and we're going to church on Sunday."

I never saw a person so "uninterested" in all my life. She said, "Well, ya'll go ahead."

I said, "No, we're all going."

She said, "I'm not."

I said, "But, Honey, today I trusted the Lord, and I want our family to get into church. We're going to start going to church."

"Well, I'm not going to church."

I said, "Yes, you are going to church!"

"I'm not going to church!"

I said, "You stay home if you want to. But I'm taking Linda and we're going to church." Boy! On Sunday morning I got Linda dressed and we took off and went to church.

I'm saved tonight because someone had a personal interest in me. I am preaching because somebody cared. Somebody prayed and somebody was faithful. If you are saved tonight, you are saved because somebody probably took a personal interest in you. Somebody called your name at Heaven's door. Somebody invited you to church.

That's why we ought to contact other people and win them one by one to Jesus. How is it that we can enjoy the benefits of the prayers and witness of others who won us to Christ and then not be interested in trying to get others saved? God help us and forgive us for our selfishness and our apathy in not trying to get somebody else saved.

People are saved because somebody is personally interested in them. Whom do you have on your prayer list? For whom are you praying? Whom have you been visiting? On whose door have you knocked week after week?

I do not know how many hours that dear deacon, Tom Koontz, spent praying for me, how many times he witnessed, how many Scriptures he read or quoted to me before I was saved. But I thank God for his personal interest. No one else in that railroad shop talked to me about being saved. No one else took a personal interest in me except Tommy Koontz.

I am reminded of the story of an elderly lady who stood one

morning in a church and gave her testimony. She had trusted Christ through reading a tract that had been given to her. It seems there was a man in her little town whose custom was to fill his pockets with tracts and go into different neighborhoods and pass out tracts and invite people to church. Each Saturday, he spent two or three hours doing this.

One particular Saturday it was raining hard. Looking at the clock and realizing that it was time for his father to leave as usual to pass out tracts, the man's son asked, "Father, aren't you going today to pass out tracts as you always do?"

His father said, "Son, the rain is pouring awfully hard. Maybe it will slack up in a little while and I'll go."

After a while the little boy said, "Would you mind if I go in your place?"

He said, "Son, it's raining hard out there."

"I know," the son replied, "but I have a raincoat and rain hat. I could go."

The father said, "Well, if you want to, you can go in my place. But don't go far."

So, the little boy got the tracts and went from door to door in the rain passing out tracts. He came to a door and knocked. No one came to the door. He knocked again and nobody came. He kept knocking and knocking and knocking. Finally, a little old lady opened the door and said, "Yes, son, what do you want?"

"Ma'am, I'd just like to give you something and invite you to come to church."

She thanked the little boy and went back inside.

The little lady continued her story in church that day, and the little boy who had given her the tract was there. She said that her husband had died a few months before. They had lived together many years. She was lonely after his death. She said that it was so lonely and so empty that she had nothing to live for. On that rainy afternoon, she had made up her mind to take her life. She had gotten a chair, had tied a rope to the ceiling and was tying it around her neck when she heard a knock. She thought, "He'll go away." But he kept knocking.

To get rid of the caller, she got down and went to the door and

asked what he wanted. He said, "I would like to give you this."
She opened the tract and read something that she did not know
before. It told her that Someone really loved her. That day, she
accepted Jesus Christ as her personal Saviour.

That woman was saved because a little boy knocked on her
door and gave her a tract. He took a personal interest in her. You
can do that. Boys and girls, you can do that. Men and women,
you can do that, too. It doesn't take a lot of effort to pass a tract
to someone, and God only knows what it will do, what life may be
changed or rearranged because someone took time to care.

II. A SECOND MIRACLE HAPPENED

I preach for two reasons: Because of a miracle and because of a
tragedy. The tragedy brought me to submission to God's will for
my life. When I rejoiced at being saved and wanted to go to
church and wanted to be baptized, my wife would have no part
in it. Consequently, after attending a few times, I said, "All
right, if you won't go, I won't go either." I thought I was being
smart. Husband, that is the wrong thing to do. Wife, that is the
wrong thing to do. Do not hold back. You go on to church. You
keep on praying. You be faithful and true to God.

I did not go to church, and the months rolled by. One day at
work I received a telephone call from the doctor for whom my
mother worked as a nurse. The doctor said, "Mr. Hancock, your
mother has been treated for a minor illness for some time, but we
have learned from X-rays that she is eaten up with cancer. There
is really no need for surgery. An operation could not help her."
Mother was fifty-one. He went on to say, "But I will admit to you
that there is a higher Power than I. There is a greater Physician
than I. All you can do is pray."

Why, that struck me like a bolt of lightning. Mother had
worked hard since my father's death. Fifty-one years of age! My
father was dead at thirty-one. These thoughts flooded my mind
as I walked away from the phone weeping. My dear friend with
whom I still worked asked, "What is the matter? What is
wrong?"

I said, "My mother is dying with cancer. The doctor told me

that there is not anything I can do but pray." I told him, "Tommy, I'm in no fit condition to be asking any favors of God. I haven't done what He wants me to do. I haven't been right with God. I'm backslidden. I got backslidden before I got started good. Who am I to be praying and asking God to do anything? Would you please tell the boss I'm gone?" I asked. "I'm leaving. I'll see you tomorrow, maybe." And I just walked out.

I didn't go to the locker room to get my clothes; I climbed into my car with my workclothes still on and went home. I told my wife, "Honey, didn't you tell me the other day that you—a couple of weeks ago—ran off two preachers?"

She said, "I did." (She was out in the yard in her shorts. Two preachers came by and she would not talk with them but sent them on their way.)

I asked, "Doesn't one of them live around here?"

"Yes, he lives right over there." She asked what was wrong and I told her.

I said, "I'm going to hunt that preacher. I have to find out how to get right and how to pray."

I knocked on his door. I told him my story. That man had never seen me before. He is one of the dearest and closest men of God I know of anywhere.

I said, "Preacher, help me get right with God if you can. Show me what to do. Tell me what to do and I will do it."

Bless his heart, he knelt with me; and we wept and prayed together; and I got right with the Lord that afternoon. Later, I shared this with my wife. We were both broken. We tried to pray. That Sunday morning we went forward in church. I said,"I'm going to take my stand for Jesus." My wife got saved. We both followed the Lord Jesus Christ in believer's baptism. We both joined the church and began to pray.

My pastor told us to pray and pray earnestly. He said, "God performs miracles, but never forget this. Pray, 'Lord, Thy will be done.' Determine right now that you are going to serve God regardless of what He does, and determine that before you enter into this prayer session."

I made up my mind. I prayed, "Lord, I don't know what You

are going to do; but I believe You can do what You said You will do, if it is Your will. But one thing, if it is not Your will to heal my mother, then keep me strong. Don't let me quit and give up and blame You for it."

I am preaching tonight because of a tragedy. I believe that it took the death of my mother to bring me to God, to bring me to the door of that preacher's home that afternoon.

Some of you are backslidden, and you know it. You know whether you are right with God or not. It may take some tragedy in your life to bring you to the place where you fall on your face and tell God you are ready to do whatever He wants and be faithful at it.

As I look back over my life, there have been many times through the years that I have thought, *O God, if I had gone on and done right, maybe my mother would be living today.* There are a lot of things that I do not know, but I know that her illness and death brought me to a place of surrender. I surrendered to preach the Gospel before she died.

By the way, my mother had not been a Christian, but she was saved during her illness. A host of others were saved as a result of the tragedy of my mother's death: my wife, my brothers, other relatives, and a multitude of friends.

My mother had very little of this world's goods. Before she died, she called her three sons to her bedside. She knew the extent of her illness and she knew she was going to die. She called me first because I was her eldest son. "Raymond, the time is near and it won't be long. Make me a promise. I only ask one thing of you. I want you to keep this promise as nearly as you can."

I said, "Mother, to the best of my ability, I will keep it. What is your wish?"

"I only want you to do this one thing. Promise me that you will be the very best Christian you know how to be."

I said, "Is that all?"

"That's all."

She called John. "John, I want you to promise me that you will be the very best Christian that you know how to be."

She called Oscar. "Oscar, I want you to promise me that you

will be the very best Christian that you know how to be."

That was all she asked.

I haven't been the best, but I have never gotten away from that nor forgotten it. Her wish has always been a challenge to my heart and life. Brother, there is a heavenly host watching, looking on; and I believe my mother is hearing me preach. She did not hear me before she died. I surrendered to preach near the close of her illness. She was confined and did not hear me preach down here, not until after she went to be with the Lord. But, I believe she has heard me preach many times since then. I preach tonight because of a tragedy.

At the beginning of my testimony, I mentioned that I preach because of a miracle, the miracle of salvation. I preach tonight because of another miracle. God is in the business of working miracles, and He performed another miracle in my life.

I have a pilot's license. I have been checked out to fly almost anything in single engine, retractable gear, controllable props— whatever. On one occasion, I was flying some men to take pictures of our church facilities, camp grounds, etc. in Florida. After landing, the men had gotten out and I was about to hangar the plane. The plane belonged to the man who owned the hangar, one whom I had led to Christ. The man, his son, and some others wanted to go up and fly. They said, "Would you take one more load up?"

I said, "I can't. I have to go to a meeting."

He said, "Please take one more load. You are in the cockpit. Take it up."

I said, "All right, but quickly. Just up and around the pattern and that's it."

So, we took off. Right over the church and over the trees the motor stopped. I said to the children and to the man sitting in the co-pilot's seat, "Be sure your safety belts are fastened; we are going to land." The kids did not know we were going to crash. A pilot has less than a minute, maybe ten to twelve seconds at the most, to decide where he is going to put that plane with no power. The only place that wasn't thickly populated with trees was a field. There was an opening to get into the field, but it had power lines and I had to cross them. I turned the plane and set it up in a glide that I hoped would cross those lines and get the plane into the field. I knew if I could get it on the ground in some fashion, I could go through a fence or ground loop it, which might tear up the plane, but we could get out all right.

I had done emergency landing before. That same plane had quit on me before, but I had then landed it safely. I set the plane into the glide. If you know anything about flying, you know a plane has to have a certain amount of speed for control. It's what we call stalling speed. This plane's stalling speed was sixty miles per hour. It was a tri-pacer. Below sixty miles an hour, controls don't mean a thing. The plane does what it wants—it just falls until it picks up speed.

I couldn't tell you in detail anything that happened other than my turning for the field and setting up the glide. I was told later about the crash. I don't remember because I had total amnesia of the crash.

A man on the ground watching the plane told me that just as the plane crossed the power lines, it reached the stalling speed and fell. There was not enough room between the power lines and ground for me to regain control and the plane fell and hit on the right side. It hit the right gear, the right wheel, then bounced over to the left wheel which collapsed and threw the nose and left wing into the ground. As the nose and left wing were twisted in the crash, my left foot, which was on the controls, was twisted and caught in the wreckage off to the left. The old safety straps gave way and sent me forward. My neck caught the wheel and my face hit the panel which crushed my nose.

In addition to cuts and bruises, hitting the wheel crushed my larynx and severed my vocal chords. The other man bumped his head, but the children escaped serious injury.

Cutting me out of the wreckage and putting me in an ambulance, the ambulance drivers stated that I would probably not live to get to the hospital. Upon arrival at the hospital, I was still alive; but the swelling in my neck cut the air from my wind pipe and an emergency tracheotomy was done to prevent suffocation.

I regained some consciousness, and I remember the doctor tell-

ing me what he would have to do. So they did the surgery on my
throat and on my leg. The next thing I could remember was being in intensive care and glad to be alive. With a tracheotomy, I
could not speak since I was breathing through it and not through
my nose. I remember writing a note and asking for a mirror so
that I could see what had happened. Of course, they would not
give me a mirror. My nose was broken and my face was a mass of
cuts and bruises.

After being moved from intensive care, the throat specialist,
Dr. Dunn, explained what had happened to my throat in the
crash and what he had done in surgery. He explained that he had
put everything back in place and had put some spacers in place
to separate the vocal chords, but that fluid would work through
the chords which could prevent them from working at all. The
right side was totally damaged with much scar tissue built up on
both sides. He stated that it was very doubtful that I would have
any voice at all for preaching or speaking. He said that my voice
was gone. He said that after six weeks the spacers would be
removed from the throat. Then, it would be determined what to
do from there.

That was the time I had to practice what I had been preaching
for a long time. That was a time that I had to say, *I think I'll just
go on anyway.*

When my wife came in, I wrote her a note telling her what the
doctor had said—that I would not be able to preach anymore.
"So it looks like you won't be married to a preacher anymore," I
wrote her. "But, you know what? I have always wanted to write
more. Now, I can write for the Lord and get out the Gospel that
way." And I meant it—I really did.

Well, my wife looked at me and said, "Preacher, you'll preach
again." I thought she was just trying to cheer me up.

My wife is a great Christian. She is a great soul winner, a great
Bible student. She spends hours in prayer. My wife went back to
my church that Wednesday night, got up before the congregation
and told them the story. Then she said, "Church members, I
want to tell you, our preacher is going to preach again. He is going to be here. He is going to preach again."

Well, I came home with a tracheotomy, a cast on my leg, and had to use a suction machine to keep the tracheotomy clean. My wife kept close track of me. She bathed me every morning and kept the tracheotomy clean. One morning, though, I felt as though I were strangling to death. And I was. . . . The spacers that had been placed in my throat had come loose and had moved and were literally choking me to death.

An ambulance rushed me to the hospital. I thought I would die before they got me there. My doctor was out of town. His assistant was called immediately. He came into the emergency room, put me on the table, hung my head over, swung the lights around, and took the spacers out of my throat.

Later, when my doctor came to see me, he said, "Preacher, I do not know what has happened. I have no explanation. I'm sorry. We will have to put the spacers back in." They got me all ready, opened up my throat and looked to see what had happened. Dr. Dunn said, "I don't believe what I see!"

I was anxious to ask him what he saw. I thought I must be nearly dead.

Again the doctor said, "I don't believe what I see!"

My wife was there and she asked, "What in the world is wrong?"

The doctor said, "Do you know that I see a perfect set of vocal chords and larynx? It can't be, but I see it!" He called his nurses in. He continued, "If I had not seen this throat myself, if I had not done the surgery myself, I could not tell that it has ever been touched."

He called in another specialist to take a look. My doctor said, "I don't believe you will be needing this thing" as he pulled the tracheotomy from the throat. It was a long metal tube, and he pulled it out. He asked his nurse for a Band-aid which he put over the hole in my throat. He said, "See if you can speak to me."

I said, "How are you doing, Doc?" And I've been at it ever since. I have never had anything but a Band-aid on my throat! And I've never had so much as to go back to the doctor for my throat. The doctor took his pen and he said, "This is not the way

I said it would turn out." Then he wrote with his pen across my file, "Closed: disgustingly healthy."

I would not make fun or mockery, but you do not have to get into a healing line to be healed. You do not have to have a prayer cloth or a prayer card. If anyone believes in divine healing, I do. But more than that, I believe in the Divine Healer. I'm here to tell you that God performed a miracle—a literal miracle—which is on the medical records in Tampa, Florida. You can go to the throat specialist, Dr. Dunn, and ask him. He will give you personal testimony of what happened. You can talk to the people in my former church in Tampa, people who went to prayer. Yes, God heals today. But, I believe we have to do it the right way, and that is God's way

I am preaching tonight, ladies and gentlemen, because of a miracle and because of a tragedy. But in it all, I'm glad to be preaching. I'm glad to be a Christian. I hope by this testimony, hearts have been encouraged. If you are a backslider and away from God, then come back to Him. Will you say, "I'm going to face up to my backslidings and go to God and tell Him I am backslidden and want His forgiveness, that I want to live for Him, that I want to serve Him, that I want Him to bless my family and my friends. I want Him to use me to personally touch some other life for Jesus"?